SHAKESPEARE

I V

1601-1605

GARETH LLOYD EVANS

OLIVER AND BOYD

EDINBURGH

OLIVER AND BOYD

Tweeddale Court
14 High Street
Edinburgh EH1 1YL
(A division of Longman Group Limited)

0 05 0023268 Hardback
0 05 002325x Paperback

Printed in Great Britain for Oliver and Boyd
by Cox & Wyman Ltd, London, Fakenham
and Reading

WRITERS AND CRITICS

||||||||||||||||||||||||||||||||||

Chief Editor

A. NORMAN JEFFARES

CONTENTS

PREFACE   vii

1 THE YEARS OF CRISIS—1601–1605   1

2 SHAKESPEARE AND TRAGEDY   16
     Hamlet   22
     Othello   44
     King Lear   61
     Macbeth   88

3 A PROBLEM TRAGEDY: 117
   Timon of Athens

   REFERENCES   129

PREFACE

This, the fourth volume of the series on Shakespeare's life and work, is concerned with the years of his preoccupation with the great Tragedies—*Hamlet, Othello, King Lear* and *Macbeth. Timon of Athens*, a puzzling play by reason of the problems relating to its dating and its authorship, is included because, in some ways, it has the quality of being a dramatic and thematic detritus left over after the volcanic imaginative activity which produced the major tragic plays.

As with the other volumes in the series discussion of the plays is accompanied by an account of Shakespeare's life during the period when he wrote them—in this volume *circa* 1601 to 1605. The emphasis of the biographical section is on factual evidence and reasonable speculation. No attempt is made to "create" a particular image of Shakespeare though it is hoped that the lineaments of a credible human being are apparent.

In the critical sections the emphasis is on the plays as pieces for performance. Frequent reference is made, therefore, both to actual performances and to the views and opinions of actors and actresses both dead and alive. The method adopted is intended to give a cohesive picture of the growth of a dramatist's genius and to cater thereby for the needs of both students and theatregoers.

The notes to each chapter incorporate a specific bibliography for each volume. A larger and more comprehensive bibliography will appear in the final volume (number five). In all quotations from the plays the original spelling and punctuation are left substantially unmodernised but it will be appreciated that, in some cases (particularly *Hamlet*) subjective editorial decisions have had to be made in the face of the existence of both Quarto and Folio texts. Thus, the texts consulted for each play are as follows. *Hamlet*—Quarto two (1604) and the Folio. The so-called "bad" Quarto of 1603 is so clearly a pirated version that it has been virtually ignored. *Othello*—both the first Quarto (1622), which is a good text, and the Folio have been consulted. *King Lear*—this play presents particular editorial difficulties in view of the doubt about the status of the first Quarto of 1608. On the other hand, the first Folio text is not without some difficulties. The most reasonable procedure is to make a judicious amalgam of both. *Macbeth*—the Folio text is the only authoritative one and is probably itself based upon a prompt copy. *Timon of Athens*—first published, so far as is known, in the first Folio. The problems surrounding this text are discussed in the chapter on the play.

The following alterations have been made silently: ampersands are expanded; short "s" is used for long "s"; "i/j" "u/v" and "w/vv" are normalised. Common Elizabethan abbreviations like yr for "your" and n for "nn" are expanded in full.

GARETH LLOYD EVANS

Stratford-upon-Avon 1971.

I

THE YEARS OF CRISIS — 1601 - 1605

Some of the greatest plays in the history of world drama were
written in the handful of years from 1601 to 1605. This space of
time also corresponds to one of the most dramatic and, in some
senses, troublesome periods in Shakespeare's own life. Indeed,
those who believe that the greatest art comes from inner tumult
may find justification in reflecting upon what is known of that life
and relating it to their experience of the plays Shakespeare wrote
then.

Certainly, conjecture plays a large part, as ever, in any investi-
gation of this period of his life, for the documented facts are few
and far between; yet it would be foolish to dismiss a recognition
of those responses which a man so sensitive as Shakespeare would
be likely to make to certain dangerous and melancholy events.
Some of these events—one in particular—touched him very
closely and privately; others, of public moment, must have come
near to him.

In these years Shakespeare's life as dramatist and as man of substance expanded—to this extent they were years of tremendous
success. Yet when we consider the possible effects of the other
private and public happenings, the question of the inner tensions
accompanying success is bound to arise. It is an unanswerable
question, though it is one we are bound to pose when we notice
the ways in which the habitual optimism of the plays he had
written up to 1598-9 is subjected to the most tremendous
strains in the so-called "problem" comedies and in the tragedies.
It is not enough to say that he had reached the highest point of his

intellectual and imaginative maturity and that, therefore, we should expect his vision of life to be more complicated, more comprehensive and, therefore, more "mixed" than before. For the "problem" plays and the tragedies suggest a crisis of the mind and spirit—a crisis of faith in humanity itself. In the late plays the faith returns, though in a different form—this return is, in itself, something of a proof that in the preceding period Shakespeare had gone through a darkness which was less part of a logical development than a terrible and mounting accretion of doubts, confusions, and anxieties. What is, however, true is that far from there being a corresponding loss of artistic energy and imaginative discipline, this period of darkness marks the height of his mastery over his craft and art.

Indeed, if it be true that Shakespeare demonstrates, at this time of his life, that great art comes from great turmoil, it may also be claimed that his tragedies confirm another generalisation. It may be that the works of Blake, Tolstoy and Shakespeare offer proofs that artists of the highest genius are only able to absorb and channel inner turmoil by a gargantuan application of imaginative discipline and technical control. A definition of the highest genius may lie in the extent to which chaos is *consciously* confronted by the forces of creative order, and is overcome by them. What is beyond argument is the presence of an ordering mind in the great tragedies. Whatever strains and stresses Shakespeare had suffered, they are never allowed, in these plays, to delete his superb professional instinct or conscious application to the writing of drama. The crisis of the mind and spirit, if it existed (and it is hard to believe that it did not), is triumphantly objectivised in dramatic terms. Whatever there may be of agonised privateness in the genesis of the plays has been transmuted into public communication. The crisis is made shareable by the exercise of professional skills which have increased rather than diminished.

Another remarkable feature of the great tragedies is that although they plumb the depths of human despair, cruelty, hatred and deception, concentrating their energies on those things in man which may destroy him intellectually, spiritually and physically, they are, none the less, magnificent affirmations of the power and beauty and dignity of the human spirit; indeed the reflection that this one man was capable of creation of this high order is, in itself, ennobling. If we remember that we can (and ought to) come away from performances of these plays exhilarated rather than put down, we are near to a proof that great art is never a denial but always an affirmation of the worthwhileness of life.

Yet, during the years of writing the tragedies, mortality was in the air, and it is in the forms it took and places where it struck that we may find grounds for a belief that behind the tragedies there lies a territory of darkness and disquiet into which Shakespeare moved.

Whatever he may have thought of Sir Thomas Lucy, and it is possible that the first speeches of *The Merry Wives of Windsor*[1] make Shakespeare's position clear, this landowning knight had been, throughout his life, something of a champion at Stratford. He had patiently and assiduously taken the side of the civic authorities in a series of encounters with Sir Edward Greville— lord of the manor of Stratford.[2] Greville took his position overzealously and interpreted his rights with injudicious severity. He had tried and failed to prevent Richard Quiney becoming bailiff, but the attempt soured his relations with both corporation and townspeople. In January 1601 he enclosed what was common pasture land on the Bancroft. This act turned local resentment into active hostility. Sir Thomas Lucy might have been able to prevent what happened, but he had died in the summer of 1600. Shakespeare must have heard, with some disquiet, of the actions of his friend and acquaintances who, with no Lucy to counsel them or persuade Greville, broke down the enclosures and drove livestock back into the pasturage. Quiney, John Sadler and Henry Walker were arrested and committed to the Marshalsea prison on Bankside. There is no record of any contact between the arrested men and Shakespeare, though Quiney did have the advice of a lawyer of the Middle Temple (Thomas Greene) who came from Warwick and had just become solicitor to Stratford Corporation.

The case of Greville versus Stratford Corporation in the matter of enclosures was to be presented in London by Quiney upon Greene's advice. The latter, moving tactfully in the direction and expectation of becoming Town Clerk of Stratford, consulted some of the older burgesses before presenting Quiney with his advice. Among them was John Shakespeare who, having lived in the shadows following his departure from public office, had by 1601 regained much of his dignity, no doubt aided by the growing affluence and reputation of his son. He steps out of the shadows with advice, and then he is gone for ever. He was buried on 8 Sept. 1601 in Holy Trinity.

William Shakespeare must surely have been in Stratford on that date. His father was dead, the town was restless, mutability surrounded him. He would have been told of the death, four months earlier, of another old man he must have known well. This was Thomas Whittington, who had for many years been a shepherd to the Hathaway family. In his will Whittington mentions the family.

> Item I geve and bequeth unto the poore people of
> Stratford 40s. that is in the hand of Anne Shaxspere,
> wyf unto Mr Wyllyam Shaxspere.[3]

One occurrence in this sad assembly of events which would have confronted Shakespeare at Stratford may have lightened his spirits for a time. Not long before John Shakespeare died a twenty-six-years-old man by the name of John Hall came to live in Stratford. He was a physician and may, indeed, have attended upon John's last illness. Whether he did or no, it is not beyond reason to believe that he met William Shakespeare and that they talked together, not merely about medicine and the world, but also about Susanna—Shakespeare's eighteen-year-old daughter whom Hall was later to marry.

The town that William Shakespeare had known as a boy was no longer the same town; many of the people he had known were gone, his own father was dead and perhaps, with a shock of surprise, he realised that his eldest daughter was now of marriageable age. Perhaps, too, he thought of Hamnet, who would have been sixteen. When we think of John Shakespeare perhaps our imaginations, almost automatically, rest upon the image of Lear or of Duncan who, after fitful fevers, slept well. It is not difficult to allow the fancy to curl around the images of those old men in the plays (particularly Lear) who, having had authority and power, make a stupid error of judgement, and lose everything though, in the end, love and dignity are restored. Critical sentiment is easily released at the notion of William Shakespeare standing at his father's graveside, seeing his own mother and sisters, meeting his daughter's future husband, and finding his imagination stirring with the as yet unformed shapes of Lear, Cordelia, Prospero, Miranda, Hermione, Perdita and Ferdinand. Critical propriety is inclined to reject the sentiment, but where else, one wonders, did Shakespeare learn so much about the domesticities of the family relationships which are embedded inside the fathers, mothers and daughters to whose creation so much of his later writing life was dedicated?

Shakespeare would have arrived at Stratford in September 1601 already worried by events of great and public concern. These events, in one degree or another, affected most people, but must have had a particular significance for him. Halliday goes so far as to say that "the death of Hamnet had been the first major crisis in Shakespeare's life, and, so far as we know, the Essex rebellion was the second".[4]

We may be certain that, in one respect, the Essex rebellion did touch Shakespeare closely. The connections between *Richard II* and the rebellion had doubtless occasioned much heart-searching and apprehension in the Lord Chamberlain's company. Some of the more fiery of Essex's supporters had asked six of the Chamberlain's Men to play it on 7 Feb. 1601 to incite the public to support Essex. There is no doubt that, in the minds of many, *Richard II* was political dynamite. Essex saw himself as a Bolingbroke who, either by persuasion or force, was to take the crown of England from Elizabeth, who had forfeited, by fecklessness and ill counsel, the right to rule—like Richard. The story of connections made between Essex and the play of *Richard II* has been told many times.[5] What is apposite to record here is the close questioning of the Lord Chamberlain's Men by the agents of Coke, the Attorney-General. Considering the assiduousness of Coke's department in pursuing treason, or even the faint smell of it, it is virtually certain that Shakespeare himself did not escape their inquiries—he was, after all, the author of the play.

He had, perhaps for the first time in his life, found himself directly and dangerously, if innocently, drawn into that great maw which always exists for artists in states whose political organisation has a low tolerance for the exercise of the free imagination. Any history play of Shakespeare's could, without over-devious manipulation, have been used by Elizabethan political activists for political ends. It appears, however, that until the Richard/Essex connection was made, Shakespeare had, either by fortune, good report or skill, steered clear of difficulty. It must have been a tremendous shock to find himself under suspicion. One effect of the Essex rebellion on him seems certain; in that year of 1601, it was probably the catalyst which, aided by later events at Stratford, first began to condition the new colouring of his imagination and spirits. "We are not safe" are words which may have run persistently through his mind as that year wore on.

The second possible effect is less certain. An acceptance of it depends much more on conjectural probability—first on the kind of man Essex was, and second on Shakespeare's opinion of him. It may be added that, if his opinion was high, Essex's death could have had a great effect on him. Dover Wilson has this to say of Essex:

> He was generous to a fault, the soul of loyalty to his friends, open and frank in manner, ever gracious and kindly to dependents, a man of wide cultural interests, a poet of some distinction, a brilliant conversationist. . . . He seemed a bundle of contradictions, to explain which baffled even the subtlest of his contemporaries.[6]

He concludes that "It was inevitable that such an enigmatic figure, so close to him, and while alive so portentous for the future of the whole state, should fascinate the greatest imagination of the age". Wilson sees an "inner pressure" in Hamlet, and claims that a re-working of the text of the play, following Essex's death, gave

> Shakespeare's final thoughts of a man at once very dear to him and very clearly judged. . . . Everything is there: his courtesy, his kindness to inferiors, his intellectual virtues, his

passion for drama, his interest in spiritualism, his open and free nature. . . .[7]

and Dover Wilson sums up by declaring that "Hamlet's mystery is the mystery of Essex".

This view has many supporters, yet a complete acceptance of the Essex/Hamlet complex must be subject to some questioning. It is unlikely that Shakespeare, whose fingers had been burnt in the fire of *Richard II*, would have been so incautious as to create, so soon after the death of a stated traitor, a picture of him so explicit and appealing that not only later scholars but also, presumably, Elizabethan audiences would find Essex there. Dover Wilson claims that "for his contemporaries it served as a revelation of the troubled spirit of the most puzzling and the most canvassed character of the time".[8] If this is true the revelation must have been immediately recognised for what it was intended to be—a sympathetic memorial to Essex. This seems an extraordinarily dangerous procedure especially if it is true, as Wilson says, that "Shakespeare loved Essex, loved him more than most and admired him, this side idolatry, as much as any".[9]

For political reasons, it seems difficult to believe that Essex and Hamlet can be identified in any explicit way. For artistic reasons, it is unbelievable that Shakespeare would commit the cardinal mistake of cleaving too closely to actuality in creating fictional character. He knew the difference between imaginative creation and direct reportage.

In the disquieting times through which he was passing, both publicly and privately, it seems likely that a subtle combination of forces pressed upon him. Within this combination the death of a shepherd, the death of John, the events at Stratford, and the execution of Essex, all played a part in forming an atmosphere, for the most part dark and cloudy, which swirled around his spirits and imagination.

We have to recall, too, that all of Shakespeare's working life up to this time had been spent in the reign of Queen Elizabeth and that, in 1601, that reign was undeniably near its end. Particular matters affected his mind and spirit and their colouring was conditioned by the state of the realm of England. In 1601 the Queen had two years to live. The approaching end was becoming very obvious to many people. For all the political astuteness which, throughout her reign, she had displayed in large and small affairs, she had also frequently displayed vacillation and an unreasonable fractiousness of temper. As she grew older her lesser qualities began to dominate the greater. Indeed, her most consistently successful achievement had been to nourish an image of herself—as Gloriana—which disguised some of the reality. It was this which both protected and raised her status as Queen of England. There were some, like Essex's supporters, who impatiently looked behind the image, and it is a measure of the dissatisfaction at what they saw that they were so pertinacious and obvious in their attempts to de-throne her. Old age not only exacerbated her weaker characteristics but, inevitably, tarnished the image itself. Moreover, even before 1601, it had become increasingly clear that she would have no children—images alone do not produce heirs.

The temperature of her realm was, therefore, chilly in 1601. Impatience with her loosening grasp of affairs, fears for the future and a kind of enervating nostalgia, combined to produce a shivering disquiet. The psychology of societies *en masse* is a slippery matter to consider, yet it may be that the coincidence of a closing reign and the end of a century added to the atmosphere. The history of countries, and certainly of England, shows that *mal de siecle* is not entirely the invention of chroniclers.

Thus mutability was in the air for the nation as well as for William Shakespeare. About 1600 he wrote *The Phoenix and the Turtle*.[10] This has been subjected to a variety of interpretations, including a suggestion that it is an evocation of the tragic love between Elizabeth and Essex. Whatever its meaning, its mood is inescapable. It is quite unlike anything else that Shakespeare wrote in pure poetic form. It has a sombre, elegiac quality, an air of total finality. There is no mitigation of its dark conclusion:

> Truth may seem but cannot be;
> Beauty brag, but 'tis not she:
> Truth and beauty buried be.

To this urn let those repair
That are either true or fair;
For these dead birds sigh a prayer.

An adumbration of the various possible reasons for the change in Shakespeare's spirits in the last two years of the sixteenth century must always lack proof. It is both easy and dangerous to say that Shakespeare wrote the problem plays and the tragedies because of certain events and circumstances—it is impossible to be sure. In any case such a critical procedure must be incomplete. The working professional dramatist will very often turn to modes and forms not merely because of inner compulsions fed by outer circumstances, but simply because the hard facts of his profession require it. A writer may, to his surprise, find what his soul is like upon such compulsions. It should be remembered that, by 1601, the boys' companies in the private theatres had become very serious rivals to the large patronised companies who were associated with the public theatres.[11] The boys had ridden into popularity upon the sensational successes of the plays associated with what is called the War of the Theatres. In 1601 nine plays were performed at the traditional revels—three of them by boys' companies.

The Chamberlain's Men must have felt the pinch. Apart from the rivalry of the boys, Shakespeare's company had to contend with the ruthlessly clever manoeuvrings of one of the greatest theatre tycoons of all time—Henslowe.[12] He, too, had suffered from the boys. His reaction was typical. He engaged in a kind of take-over bid which very much strengthened his position—at the expense of the Chamberlain's Men. He let the Rose Theatre to Worcester's Men and completed a contract with them similar to the one he had with the Admiral's Men at the Fortune. The effect of this contract was to make the actors virtually bound to him personally. For example, he advanced to the Admiral's Men enough money to pay their working debts and kept a strict account of his outlay and of the repayments made to him by instalment. He sometimes loaned money to actors which they also repaid in instalments. By such means, in a profession whose attention to financial minutiae and to the virtue of thrift is not renowned, he became a kind of financial overlord. In 1601 when he completed the contract with Worcester's Men, he tacitly increased his overlordship of the London theatres. Moreover, he had "bound" to him a fine collection of actors, including Kempe, and one first-rate playwright—Thomas Heywood. Under his astute management the combined Worcester's and Admiral's company performed at the Rose Theatre—within spitting distance from the Globe where the Lord Chamberlain's Men struggled with adversity.

The compulsion for Shakespeare to write *Hamlet* and other plays may well have involved the necessity to repair the Globe's dented fortunes. *Hamlet* seems to have been a hit. Scoloker described it as a play that "should please all";[13] it was performed twice on board ship bound for India. It had Richard Burbage in the leading part, and enough violent death to satisfy any audience which remembered, with relish, the gory pleasures of Kyd's *The Spanish Tragedy*.[14] It had, of course, much more for the perceptive, but theatre then, as now, made its money less from the perceptive than from the unsophisticated.

By 1602 the position had eased—a measure of this is that the Chamberlain's Men presented the first production at the revels in December. And in this year Shakespeare began a series of negotiations connected with land in Stratford which clearly imply that he had either not suffered much financially or had recouped swiftly from the lean days at the Globe in the previous year.

On 1 May 1602, a deed[15] was executed by William and John Combe relating to the purchase of 107 acres of arable land, with appurtenances, by William Shakespeare. The deed is not signed by the dramatist, presumably because he was not in Stratford, but it was sealed and delivered to his brother, Gilbert. The price paid was £320, and this may very well have been in cash since there is no evidence that any mortgage was taken out for the sale. The land lay within "the parrishe feilds or towne of Olde Stretford" and it included common pasture for sheep, horses and pigs. It is necessary to be clear about certain points. First, this purchase confirms Shakespeare's financial affluence; second, the extent and position of the land gave him not only a strong economic status but a social eminence in Stratford; third, the deed was a "conveyance" which did not provide him, automatically, with absolute title. This was a normal procedure. Absolute title was conferred later with the deposition of a "Fine", but this did not occur until 1611. The nine-year gap may be explained by the fact that some very hard bargaining between Shakespeare and the Combes had ensued over twenty acres of land whose part in the original conveyance is implied rather than explicit. It is certainly true that the entitlement of 1611 specifies 127 (not 107) acres of land in the sale. The niceties of legal argument have woven their possibilities and imponderables around the matter of the twenty acres' discrepancy. No final legal answer seems possible, yet two conjectures concerning the nine-year gap between conveyance and completion seem feasible. The first is that if there were quibbling about the twenty acres in addition to, or as a "hidden" part of the stated 107, Shakespeare eventually won his point. It argues for a stern obstinacy in business matters. The editor of *Shakespeare Documents*[16] writes:

> The legal procedure in this action (i.e. 1611) specifically aimed at leaving no possibility whatever of error as to his title to the 20 acres. William Shakespeare, head of the family after his father's death in 1601, definitely intended that to the real estate comprising the family estate there should be clear legal title.

The second conjecture is that the nine-year gap was due to Shakespeare's inability to be resident in Stratford for the length of time required to complete the conveyance. Indeed, neither conjecture contradicts the other. We catch, perhaps, a glimpse of the son of obstinate old John Shakespeare, shrewd on commodity and dealing, waiting until he could spend enough time in his home town to conclude his certain advance into the realm of the landed gentry. He had already bought New Place in May 1597. The house had two large gardens and two barns and it had cost him £60. It was one of the largest houses in the town and it stood until 1702, when Sir John Clopton rebuilt on the site. Its position is of some interest in the light of the negotiations Shakespeare began in

1602 and completed nine years later. It had a commanding position on the right angle formed by two joining roads—Chapel
Street and Chapel Lane. On two sides, therefore, it overlooked
thoroughfares along which the Stratford citizenry would frequently walk. In September 1602 Shakespeare took steps which
suggest that he wanted to emphasise the idea of "estate". He
obtained the copyhold tenure of a cottage in Chapel Lane. The
sale involved one quarter of an acre of land. A notable point is
that, with its purchase, the property belonging to William Shakespeare now overlooked the citizens of Stratford from both sides of
their avenue to the river. Furthermore, if they lived right at the
bottom of Chapel Lane, near the river, they would, by walking
only a few hundred yards parallel to the river, arrive at the plot of
107 acres which everyone must have known John Shakespeare's
son was in process of buying from the Combes. Whether the
cottage in Chapel Lane was required for servants or for his
brothers, is not known. However, the total amount of property
belonging now to the Shakespeare family was very considerable,
and their standing in the town must have been correspondingly
high.

The accession of James I to the throne in 1603 must have had a
double-edged significance for Shakespeare. Like many others he
must have wondered, not without apprehension, what the new
reign would bring. On the other hand, he would have been less
than human had he not realised that the death of the patron of his
company (Lord Hunsdon) shortly after James's accession was not
altogether unfortunate. One of the first acts of James's reign was to
issue a royal warrant in which he himself became the patron of the
erstwhile Lord Chamberlain's Men:

> Know ye y^t we of our speciall grace certaine knowledge &
> meere motion have licenced and authorised & by these
> presentes doe license & authorise these our servantes
> Lawrence ffletcher William Shakespeare Richard Burbage
> Augustine Phillippes John Hemming Henry Condell
> William Sly Robert Armyn Richard Cowlye and the rest of
> their associates, freely to use and exercise the Arte and

facultie of playing Comedies Tragedies Histories Enterludes
Moralles Pastoralles Stage plaies & such other like as they
have already studied or hereafter shall use or studie.[17]

The warrant was followed by letters patent on 19 May 1603. They
must have rejuvenated the spirit of the Lord Chamberlain's Men.
From this time they acted with royal commission. This, automatically, gave them a status a cut or two above their rivals. In a
less abstract sense it meant much to them. Between 1603 and 1616
(when Shakespeare died) the King's Men, as they were now
known, were at Court at least 187 times. In 1604, in an account of
the Master of the Wardrobe, grants of cloth are recorded to them
—they were now entitled to wear the King's livery.

   In the midst of this accession of honour Shakespeare was still
busy about his own affairs. It is indeed extraordinary to imagine
the man, involved in the work of his company, conceiving and
writing some of his greatest plays, as still having time to attend to
commodity. In 1604, at the Court of Record in Stratford, one
Philip Rogers was summoned on complaint of debt by William
Shakespeare. He owed £1 15s. 10d. The summons detailed the
affair: March 27 1604, three measures of malt—6s.; April 10 1604,
four measures of malt—8s.; April 24 1604, three measures of
malt—6s.; May 3 1604, four measures of malt—8s.; May 16 1604,
four measures of malt—8s.; May 30 1604, two measures of malt—
3s. 10d. (the price had gone up). On 25 June Rogers borrowed two
shillings. The grand total of £2 11s. 10d. was reduced by a repay-
ment by Rogers of six shillings. Shakespeare's lawyer also asked
for a sum of 10s. being the amount to cover Shakespeare's injury
(that is, his inconvenience).

   Some historians have discounted this document on the grounds
that it may refer to another William Shakespeare—not the
dramatist. E. K. Chambers,[18] however, has shrewdly revealed that
any other William Shakespeare likely to have been involved does
not appear in local records until 1620. Moreover, there is nothing
in the transactions revealed by the summons to eliminate the
strong probability that it is the dramatist who is involved. It must
be recalled that in February 1598, during a wheat shortage in

Stratford, the dramatist was listed as having eighty bushels of corn in hand, and was described as an "engrosser and forestaller" (in modern terms a capital investor and a speculator). It has also been suggested that the dramatist was the only Shakespeare rich enough to sell Philip Rogers the quantity of malt involved. He would not have needed to be in Stratford as a witness in the case; the chances are that the shrewd man of business, meticulous about detail (note the careful enumerating of amounts and dates), sent peremptory instructions to his lawyer.

> If the documentary evidence shows anything in the case of William Shakespeare, it demonstrates that the dramatist was a shrewd business man.[19]

Although the direct evidence about Shakespeare's life and activities in this period from the turn of the century to 1605 is characteristically meagre, it may be suggested that we get a clearer portrait than at any other time of his life of the outlines of his existence. As an artist his grip upon his imagination and his craft became stronger and stronger. As a man who, during these years, became head of his family, his grip on worldly affairs does not seem to have been any less firm. As a subject, first of a dying Queen, then of a King whose disposition was unknown to the majority, he went through crisis and emerged triumphant in both status and creative power. As a family man he suffered loss and perhaps some joy.

All the speculation about the "crises" which sparked off the problem plays and the tragedies, about the Essex relationship, about his feelings on the death of his father and of his Queen, should not fail to pay attention to these four elements. From them emerges a man of tremendous balance—able to walk between the world within him and the world about him, and able to know both, without either compromise of stance or failure of nerve. We may guess that he was, in one sense, very much his father's son, hard in bargaining, unerringly firm in negotiation, avid for right and advantageous dealing. He may not, indeed, have been a particularly attractive man to do business with—no business man who seems not to put a foot wrong ever is; he may have seemed arrogant, a little upstartish in his native town, but few prodigals ever return or visit their birthplaces without seeming so to some. On the other hand, those who knew his works would be well aware that the world of his imagination was that of a civilised, honest and judicious man. The "mystery" about the personality of William Shakespeare, at this time of his life, is not so much a matter of how he could be both artist and man of the world, but the extent to which he was both. This extent suggests that he was a rare being capable of turning his immense creativity to any matter, succeeding in it, and then turning again, energy utterly undiminished.

2

SHAKESPEARE AND TRAGEDY

Unlike so many of his commentators and critics, Shakespeare was no theorist. He responded to experience with a natural urgency and transformed it into imaginative truth without striving to conform to convention or rule, in form or expression. If he had been a conformist his tragic plays would doubtless have embodied an acceptance of Aristotelian rules. They do not. The spirit of a Shakespearean tragedy is essentially different from that of Greek tragedy. Moreover, he did not find it necessary to demonstrate the authority of Aristotle by resorting, for example, to the Unities or to the ubiquitous tragic chorus.

It is well to take note of this before embarking upon any attempt to designate the nature of Shakespeare's tragic view, and its communication. Surprisingly often, his tragedies have been judged from a peculiarly grudging standpoint—suggesting that they are departures from an accepted Aristotelian pattern, and so much the worse for them. Thomas Rymer speaks most cogently for this opinion:

> In tragedy he appears quite out of his element; his Brains are turn'd, he raves and rambles, without any coherence, any spark of reason, or any rule to controul him, or set bounds to his phrenzy.[1]

Yet it is Alexander Pope who reminds us with force that there is another way of looking at it:

> To judge therefore of Shakespear by Aristotle's rules, is like trying a man by the laws of one country, who acted under those of another.[2]

Only in his apprentice days did Shakespeare show any conscious subservience to classical tragic models. The debt of *Titus Andronicus* to Seneca has been noted, yet one of the most notable features of that play is the indication it gives of a movement of Shakespeare's imagination—a pulling-away from fixed conventions. He goes, so to say, into the territory of Seneca, but very quickly emerges on the other side, tentatively flexing his own muscles.

Again, his early comedies show the effects of Commedia dell'-Arte character types and plot-lines, but it is Shakespeare's own inventions which vivify the plays.

The scholarly investigations of the sources of Shakespeare's tragic patterns are prodigious, both in number and in theory. His debt to medieval drama, to classical drama, to Renaissance "humanism",[3] have been copiously audited. The net result of these investigations has been a valuable indication of possibilities and a revelation of certain specific debts. Yet none of them, either alone, or in consort, really deliver the true coinage of the tragic plays. For all the profit that has accrued from asking the question, "Who and what influenced Shakespeare's tragedies?", it remains token payment compared with what is gained by asking the question, "What is our experience of the tragedies?"

Life is more important than death. This is Shakespeare's passionate message both to his own world and to ours. He had long contemplated the alternative, in his so-called "problem" plays. His tragedies accept the irony that the fact of life implies the inevitability of death, but it is the first part of the proposition that he is most concerned with. Hamlet, King Lear, Othello, and Macbeth suffer, in the end, the common fate of all human kind, yet this is as nothing compared with the force of life which each one of them generates on his journey towards doom. Shakespeare's interest in what happens after death is merely implied: almost off-handedly, we are made to feel that there is a reward for the good and damnation for the wicked. He does not tie his tragedies to the Christian myth. Because of this we do not, as members of an audience (although we may in the study), become involved in questions about Christian dogma as, for example, the nature of sin and its possible redemption in the after-life.

What captures our hearts and imaginations is the spectacle of lonely men, capable of conscious thought, deep feeling and willed action, trying to assert their grip on the fact of being alive. In Shakespeare's tragedies lies a most affirmative statement about the sheer importance of man—alive. This is the first and most compelling magnetism of these plays. We leave the theatre shrived of that pessimism which tells us that life is not worth living. We are, on the contrary, restored to accept the proposition that it is the very irony, cruelty, hardness, of being alive which confirm the necessity to live life to the full.

This proposition is not presented in a straight, didactic fashion; it is not bright-eyed optimism. Its force derives, to a large extent, from the fact that it is presented dramatically and with verbal splendour. Indeed, it might be said that life is worth living if only because we can experience these plays.

Drama exists only by contrasts—by the pull and push of opposites. In order that we may feel exhilarated, and not a little ennobled, by the fact of being alive, we have also, in the tragedies, to be chastened, frightened and conscience-stricken by examples of life's other colouring. We cannot accept the lonely and gracious sacrifice of Hamlet without experiencing his stubborn, self-indulgent indeterminacy. We cannot admire Lear's acquisition of wisdom, without journeying with him through his disordering blindness. We cannot feel Othello's proud sense of self and of love without being taught to condemn his folly. And (the greatest testimony of all to the exciting effects of dramatic contrast) we cannot, at the last moment, when the head of tyranny is displayed before us, condemn Macbeth peremptorily, because we remember the reckless courage that prompted him to try and remain alive against augury and circumstance.

These characters affect us because of the powerful disposition of opposites both within and without them. It is not so much the question of whether they are good men *or* evil men, which engages us, but the fact that they have elements of both qualities in them. More than this, they engage us because these mixed qualities are so large in appearance. The natural courage, the conscience, the moral compunctions of Macbeth loom as large as his evil ambitions, his cunning and his cruelty. Hamlet's princeliness, intellectual strength and emotional sensitivity are as great as his self-indulgence and emotional instability. Lear's physical and spiritual courage, his intermittent tenderness, are not less apparent than his unthinking anger, his intellectual caprice. Othello's nobility of bearing and spirit, his martial bravery, his honesty, are as affecting as his pitiable gullibility, mental instability and cruelty.

It is because opposed sets of qualities are presented in these men in such large proportions that they are able to envelop our imaginations so completely. The "tragedy" of these plays has its effect upon us less because these men die and are, directly or indirectly, the cause of death for others, than because of the irony of our witnessing the worse set of characteristics relentlessly overcoming the better. Our tragic experience is, indeed, less closely associated with the dramatic action of the whole play, than with the singular action within the tragic hero.

We naturally think of them as tragic heroes rather than as tragic villains—this is important. They are heroic in the accepted sense because what they embody in mind, imagination and action is on such a vast scale, and because the catastrophes involved are so widespread in their effects. Yet, although death and catastrophe are caused by them, we cannot classify them as villains. Foolish, misled self-indulgent, intermittently unbalanced they may be, to an inordinate extent, but our minds baulk at final and complete condemnation. Even Macbeth, the most relentlessly cruel of them all, leaves us, at the end, with an ineradicable, if grudging, access of admiration—because of his immense, stark, and fruitless courage. If it were simply the courage of a trapped and vicious brute, we would have no hesitation in condemning him out of hand. Yet at the last we remember that Macbeth has suffered the agony of having not only to fight a better self, but of being tortured by his own terrifying imagination. It is this, human, self-knowledge that rescues him for us.

They may also be absolved from the judgement of absolute villainy because they are placed in situations which test them beyond the breaking-point and over which they eventually lose all control. We encounter them at a crisis point in the most severe sense. The drama which excites us as we witness the clash within them is heightened by our realisation that the events of the plays are of a uniquely critical kind. It is as if we meet these men at the one and only point in their lives when all the lines of temperament, fate and circumstance, join. It is, indeed, as if we were at the birth of a totally unique catastrophe.

This quality of special circumstance—giving the heroes something of the posture of victims—also serves to give them a very particular status of loneliness. It is they, and they alone, who have to meet the ultimate and fatal implications of the crisis. Others, of course, are meshed into the dark pattern and their lives are changed or, indeed, ended. Yet none of the other characters in a Shakespeare tragedy ever seem to be facing the full consequences of the crisis—where, in addition to actual catastrophe, the whole personality is tested, tortured and, above all, ruthlessly exposed.

Some of them come near to this—Gloucester, Macduff, Claudius, Michael Cassio—yet we feel that they are spun about on the edges of a whirlpool whose dark centre reaches down to depths that only one man—the tragic hero—really enters. In a very certain sense these other characters, much as they suffer, exist to minister to our experience of the tragic hero; they are second-class citizens of the tragic world.

The solitariness of the tragic hero at the centre of the whirlpool increases the tragic experience for us. There is a terrible poignancy in contemplating a total loneliness of the spirit and the imagination. In crude terms we may say that these men are on their own—with themselves. Hamlet's reaching out for the comfort of Horatio only serves to convince us that there is little that Horatio can do for him; Lear's fumbling to find the hands of the Fool and of Mad Tom and, eventually, of Cordelia, is a gesture which only too piercingly confirms that he is in an agony of mind and spirit no touch of hands can divine or comprehend; Macbeth's removal from any real human association (including, eventually, that with his wife) gives us ample proof that he is journeying upon seas of the imagination no one else can compass; Othello is ironically and irretrievably solitary at those very times when he seems closest to human relationship—when he is with Iago.

The victims of the events—those second-class citizens—do not give us the experience of total isolation. Perhaps Gloucester and Lady Macbeth come closest to it, but there is an important qualification.

Out of Lady Macbeth's lonely and shattered state there come few of those profound intimations and revelations about the battle that is being fought inside the personality which is typically unique to the tragic heroes. "The Thane of Fife had a wife, where is she now?", she asks. "All the perfumes of Arabia will not sweeten this little hand," she cries, and we are aware of conscience and fear. Her husband however, in his loneliness, takes us fathoms further into the deeps of what his conscience is, what his fear is. She describes, he creates them for us.

Again, Gloucester's loneliness, given a pathetic emphasis by his blindness, is intensely affecting, but it is little more than that. His deprivations, his victimisation by filial ingratitude, is a close *obbligato* to Lear's case. Yet it is Lear, not Gloucester, who is the greatest demonstrator of the reality of suffering.

In any case these tragic heroes are larger than anything around them. Larger, not only because of the scale of their personalities, but for another reason. They above all breed in us the belief that they embody universal qualities—both good and bad. As we watch them we are not only in the presence of Hamlet the Dane, the Thane of Cawdor, the dispossessed King, the proud blackamoor General, but of archetypes, who are part of ourselves. It is a simple, perhaps hackneyed, but certain fact that they have all come to stand for certain human verities. Hamlet and melancholy have become synonymous, as have Macbeth and wicked ambition, Lear and aged folly, Othello and tragic jealousy. They are all interchangeable with the abstractions they have come to embody. We do not make the same automatic and categorical associations with the other characters in the tragedies. These tragic heroes are not only larger than life—they are massive emblems of certain unchanging and, indeed, familiar qualities in the human animal.

Yet unique as they are in the power of their dramatic presence, monopolistic as they certainly are of our attentions, they do, within the plays, inhabit a world. They stalk it, set traps for it, and shake its ground. When they leave it, it is with the force of super-beings. The different worlds of each tragedy are literally dis-ordered because these men have inhabited them. Shakespeare's great theme—the demonstration of the effects of order and dis-order—which, in one way or another, informs all his plays, abides in these tragedies. Yet, since completing the cycle of histories, he had widened and reorientated his comprehension of the meanings of disorder. His obsession with individual character—most explicitly announced in *Richard III*—had, one suspects, grown in phase with a realisation that disorder within the state is paralleled and summed up in brief by disorder within the single human be-ing. Ulysses's famous speech in *Troilus and Cressida*, long utilised by scholars to confirm their view of Shakespeare's conception of order and disorder within the political matrix, can equally be taken as a perfect general description of what happens within the com-monwealth of individual personality, of what, in fact, happens to Hamlet, Othello, Lear, and Macbeth.

A balance of forces is upset and "hark what discord follows". The world of the tragedies is one of total disorder within and with-out, but by now Shakespeare had become more interested in the inner catastrophe.

Hamlet

A young man, in black doublet and hose, a white and collared shirt, opened wide to reveal his breast; around his neck hangs a pen-dant with a miniature; the hair is awry, the eyes deep, searching, and passionate; the movements are graceful, the voice melodious, but never far away from the tones of grief and bewilderment. This, perhaps, is the most prevalent image of the character of Hamlet the Dane which has lodged in the imaginations of countless readers and theatregoers through the decades. Any departure from this, by an actor, seems always to occasion surprise —as if a fact of nature had been interfered with. A scrap of evidence about the appearance of an early Hamlet—perhaps Richard Bur-bage—suggests that the image is not perhaps after all a romantic fantasy. Antony Scoloker in his poem *Daiphantus or the Passions of Love* (1604) refers to the actor who

> Put off his cloathes; his shirt he onely weares,
> Much like mad-*Hamlet*; this as Passion Teares.

The illustrations which exist of Betterton's way and Garrick's way of presenting the part visually also suggest that they did not entirely abandon what some would call this romantic image. Yet it is the illustrations of Henry Irving's Hamlet[4] which, more than anything else, in comparatively modern times, give credence to the image. The gaunt pale face, the slim body, the black suit and open shirt. His hair was described as "black" and "disordered", it was "carelessly tossed about the forehead, but the fixed and rapt attention of the whole house is directed to the eyes of Hamlet: the eyes which denote the trouble—which tell of the distracted mind. Here are the 'windy suspiration of forced breath', 'the fruitful river in the eye', the 'dejected haviour of the visage'." This is the ur-Hamlet of our imaginations, and countless actors over the centuries have, apparently willingly, succumbed to it.

It is worth considering the reasons why this embodiment of Hamlet should be, so to say, the received one. What, in fact, is involved? The black suggests mourning and melancholy; the open white shirt suggests not only distraction but, paradoxically, a kind of romantic insouciance. The tousled hair suggests active engagement with mental problems. The beautiful voice we expect to hear conjures up the idea of a poet; the grace of movement we anticipate from the limbs within the suit, ministers to our expectation of princeliness, of an awareness of a being cutting a figure of grace and beauty across the air. Indeed, it may all add up to the conclusion that, in a certain sense, we are in the presence of a sensitive artist—one who wrestles with chaos, yet who, in his speech, his tones, his actions, tries to give that chaos not only a local habitation and a name, but one that is calculatedly formal and excitingly beautiful.

There is a unique and very particular relationship between any actor who performs Hamlet, and the part itself. With the other

great tragic heroes we always have a sense that the actor's funda-
mental problem is to enter into the character; with Hamlet, we
have a sense that the actor's problem is to control the extent and
the nature of the way in which the character enters into him. The
character of Hamlet is a direct challenge to the very core of what
we call the actor's art—fluency of expression in face and eyes,
grace and correctitude in the movements of the limbs, an infinitely
variable melodiousness of voice, an overall necessity to seem at one
and the same time pleasingly vulnerable to and dominant over the
moods and predilections of spectators. All these qualities are those
of the character and they are, of course, all the qualities which are
required of any actor who is more than an impersonator or ex-
ploiter of personality. What Hamlet expects from the actor is,
curiously, what we expect, all the time, of Hamlet,

> . . . . . whose end both at the first and
> now, was and is, to hold as 'twer the
> Mirrour up to Nature.
> [III. II. 23–5]

The greatest actors have always exemplified the truth of Hamlet's
words not only in their awareness of their own art, but in the
way in which they have conceived and embodied Hamlet the
Dane. The Prince would, we can believe, have applauded the correct projections of Garrick, as described by a contemporary. The
potent grace of presence, the willed artistry which we expect from
Hamlet seems present here.

> When Horatio says, "Look, my lord, it comes!" Garrick
> turns sharply, and at the same moment staggers back two or
> three paces with his knees giving way under him; his hat
> falls to the ground and both his arms, especially the left are
> stretched out nearly to their full length, with the hands
> nearly as high as the head, the right arm more bent, the hand
> lower, and the fingers apart; his mouth is open; thus he
> stands, rooted to the spot, with legs apart, but no loss of
> dignity. . . .[5]

Academic and insoluble speculations as to whether the hero is mad, is in love with Ophelia, has an "Oedipus complex", is dilatory, is really "fat and scant of breath", have to give place to the one undeniable effect of Hamlet upon an audience—that he is a man of civilised mind, emotional sensibility, grace of speech and movement; in fact combining many of the attributes of what is conventionally known as "the artistic temperament". This emblematic figure of the artist spans the centuries, signally lonely, singularly articulate, frequently misunderstood, but always saying something to mankind which it only faintly hears and fugitively understands. The most lasting impression left by the play, after we may have ceased to care about the immediate fate of Hamlet or anyone else in Denmark, is the feeling of having been in the presence of that fragile grace of the artist, which is for ever vulnerable in a world still impervious to civilising influences.

In a very precise sense Hamlet's dilemma is that of the artist who is required to come to close terms with reality—to enter into it too committedly at the expense of his artistic sense; the man of imagination, who places more validity on the unreal than on the real, is trapped.[6] A merely cursory glance at the play's events supports this contention. Hamlet is, in a way, most himself when by himself—when he can isolate himself from the snarls of reality, and exercise his particular artistic gifts in order to distil and comprehend, in an imaginative way, the meaning of what is happening to him and others. At several points he recoils from engagement, not because he is simply a dilatory man, but because his temperament is such that actual engagement is of less consequence to him than the imaginative conclusions that he can draw from the contemplation of action. His "explanation" for not killing Claudius at prayers, has a kind of logic about it, but this impresses us less than the manner in which he communicates himself. His "rejection" of Ophelia in the nunnery scene is compact of anger, grief, and despair, yet it cannot be denied that it is the extraordinary figure that his imagination cuts which magnetises us. His "baiting" of Polonius confirms, certainly, his decision to put on an antic disposition, but what is most remarkable is the consummate skill with which the baiting is executed.

The truth of the matter is, that as the play proceeds in

B

performance, we witness a number of manifestations of Hamlet; sober-suited, grief-racked Prince; sardonic respondent to mother and uncle; urgently intimate semi-confidant of Horatio; distracted man of passion with Ophelia; wryly witty ex-student with Rosencrantz and Guildenstern; masterful, almost gay *aficionado* of the theatrical arts with the players—and so on. This is, indeed, what happens in *Hamlet*—a dazzling variety of images are presented to us. The common denominator of all the images that are presented is that they all, to some extent, bespeak a conscious creating of the particular image at the particular time. It is, indeed, as if what we see of Hamlet throughout the play is a literal proof of the words which he speaks to Horatio after the visitation of his father's ghost.

> But come,
> Here as before, never so helpe you mercy,
> How strange or odde so ere I beare my selfe;
> (as I perchance heerafter shall thinke meet to put an
>   Anticke disposition on:)
> That you at such time seeing me, never shall
> With armes encombred thus, or thus, head shake;
> Or by pronouncing of some doubtfull Phrase;
> As well, we know, or we could and if we would,
> Or if we list to speake; or there be and if there might,
> Or such ambiguous giving but to note,
> That you know ought of me.
>
> [I. v. 168–79]

The "reality" of the situation is that Hamlet knows his mother has married hastily with his uncle, that the visitation of the Ghost confirms the prompting of his "prophetic soul" that something foul has been committed; yet his reaction is immediately to warn Horatio not to seem surprised if he finds Hamlet acting in a manner "unreal" in relation to situation and event. The conscious artist who wishes to exercise his will over his own appearance, his own attitude to events, has taken over. If we inquire what kind of artistic imagination it is that this most brings to mind, we are surely forced to the conclusion that it is the actor's. Granville Barker[7] again is helpful at this point. He writes:

> A large part of the technical achievement of Hamlet lies in the bringing home his intimate griefs so directly to us. In whatever actor's guise we see him he is Hamlet, yet the appeal is as genuine as if the man before us were making it in his own person.

This is as much as to say that the actor's temperament and the character of Hamlet are consanguineous.

It has been noted how, in both Prince Hal and in Richard III, there is a large element of that kind of dissimulation which we associate with the art of the actor. Both Hal and Richard,[8] in their very different ways, "put on" an antic disposition in order to achieve their purposes. They attempt to create the reality they desire by exercising the art of illusion. Hal "puts on", deliberately, a "loose behaviour", Richard self-consciously congratulates himself on his ability to change shape with the chameleon. It is, indeed, remarkable how baulked we can be, when we ask ourselves what is the true nature of the personalities of characters like Hal, Richard and the Fools (all of whom have this quality of dissimulation). We can, of course, say that Hal is ambitious, Richard evil, that the Fools are wittily wise, but their talent for a kind of disguise is so developed, that the final revelation of their personalities is really denied to us. We can give chapter and verse about Othello and Macbeth and Lear's personalities—why they believe in such and such a way and for what reason. Our minds, however, are made to slide off these other men, just as so often, when we meet an actor, we are unable to declare—yes, this man is like this or like that. Now, he is here, now he is gone; now he is this, now that. So it is with Hamlet. All the baffling questions we ask about motivation, about the true condition of his mind, his attitude to Ophelia, to his mother, are utterly unanswerable, because all the apparent contradictions we experience when we see Hamlet are, in fact, not contradictions at all—they are examples of the acting temperament.

The evidence of Hamlet's cleaving to the histrionic is both

varied and abundant. His immediate decision to put on an antic disposition is followed, very soon, by two pieces of evidence that he is very capable of such a putting on. He baits Polonius as a great Fool would bait an oaf. He is indeed become the witty Fool, whose jokes and taunts bear along with them the strain of truth. That his putting on, in this scene, is a conscious act of will, consciously controlled, is sharply underlined by his comment after Polonius's departure:

> These tedious old fooles.

This has all the sardonic effect of the great actor, who having bent his audience to his magic fingers, bows with mock humility, then behind the fallen front curtain, lifts up two insulting fingers to his hidden victims. Again, he has appeared, we are told, before Ophelia

> With his doublet all unbrac'd,
> No hat upon his head; his stockings foul'd,
> Ungartred and downe gived to his Anckle
> Pale as his shirt, his knees knocking each other.
> [II. I. 78–80]

What has occurred, she describes in detail.

> He tooke me by the wrist, and helde me hard;
> Then goes he to the length of all his arme;
> And with his other hand thus o're his brow,
> He fals to such perusall of my face,
> As he would draw it.
> [II. I. 87–91]

The announcement of the arrival of the players to Elsinore provides another opportunity to show us, in a now more objective, less involved way, Hamlet's intimacy with the world of the actor. He inquires if they hold the same reputation as they once did; he has strong views on the child actors who are rivalling the adults for public acclamation; he welcomes them all as friends, but one, in particular, as an old friend; even Polonius is constrained to forget

his bafflement, and to exclaim, when Hamlet speaks a speech,
" 'Fore God, my lord, well spoken, with good accent and dis-
cretion." His warm respect for the profession is definite.

> Do ye heare, let them be well us'd: for they are
> the Abstracts and breefe Chronicles of the time.
> After your death, you were better have a bad Epitaph
> than their ill report while you lived.
>> [II. II. 517–19]

His speech to the players (so much o'er-scanned by scholars
seeking to find the heart of Elizabethan acting-practice) is of
that kind which bespeaks a close relationship with the actuality of
performance. He knows the commodity involved in being a
member of an acting-company.

> I heard thee speak me a speech once, but
> it was never Acted: or if it was, not above
> once, for the Play I remember pleas'd not
> the Million, 'twas *Caviarie* to the Generall.
>> [II. II. 428–431]

It is the enactment of a play that, he believes, will "catch the
conscience of the king", for he has observed before (and closely)

> That guilty Creatures sitting at a Play,
> Have by the very cunning of the Scoene,
> Bene strooke so to the soule, that presently
> They have proclaim'd their Malefactions.
>> [II. II. 585–8]

This far, there can be little doubt about the fact that Hamlet is a
willing suitor to the world of the theatre. The extent of his com-
mittal to it involves us, however, in deeper reaches. Hamlet tells
the Queen

> That I essentially am not in madnesse,
> But mad[e] in craft.
>> [III. IV. 187–8]

The bewildered Polonius himself cogitates on the seeming fact that "though this be madness, yet there's method in't". Hamlet's actions puzzle Elsinore; it is as if the various claims that are made that he is mad have a reserve clause to them, much as Kent, in *King Lear*, is dimly aware that "this is not altogether fool, my lord". Members of Elsinore's court seem to harbour in their minds the idea that this is not altogether madness, my lord. The authority of R. W. Chambers[9] is impressive at this point. Discussing the question, "Was Hamlet, at any time and in any sense, really mad?" he writes,

> It has been held, sometimes with much learning of the alienist, that in course of time, under the strain of the situation, the pretence adapted as a mask passed into a reality. I do not think that the text, fairly read, supports this theory, and in the abstract it is surely untenable. Psychology, indeed, is hard put to it to establish a rigid dividing-line between the sane and the insane. The pathologist may distinguish certain abnormal conditions of brain-areas and call them diseased; or the lawyer may apply working tests to determine the point at which restraint of the individual liberty becomes necessary in public interests. But beyond that you cannot go.

And later on he adds,

> only of one thing we may be sure. Shakespeare did not mean Hamlet to be mad in any sense which would put his actions in a quite different category from those of other men. How could it be so, since the responsibility of the free agent is of the essence of psychological tragedy, and to have eliminated Hamlet's responsibility would have been to divest his story of humanity and leave it meaningless.

Within the context of Chambers's words, it is apposite to reflect on the fact that both Othello and Lear show more evidence of what, in modern psychiatric parlance, would be called "abnormal conditions", yet we would never consider making, with any certainty, the judgement upon them that they are "mad". We talk of a temporary distraction of their mental faculties, and we justify what we say by reflecting on the fact that these men have been driven to this condition, rather than that it is a "disease" of the mind. As Chambers says, the text, fairly read, cannot support the theory of a diseased mind. On the contrary it supports the idea of a particular kind of mind and imagination which is given to histrionics.

At the same time it is folly to attempt to explain Hamlet's behaviour merely on the basis described up to now. Once an actor has played a part he moves on to the next one. But Hamlet is a particular kind of actor—there is a continuing set of themes in every "role" which he plays during the course of the play. He is, so to speak, trying to mutate reality by taking up histrionic postures, yet, at the same time, there is that within him which refuses to be translated, however hard Hamlet tries, into mere image, shadowplay.

The most dominant tones in Hamlet's speeches are wryness and irony; these are sometimes harmonised with melancholy, with gaiety, with wit, sometimes with emotional fury, sometimes with bleak despair—but whatever the note struck, at any time, these two elements of wryness and irony are present. They appear upon his first entrance.

A little more than kin, and lesse than kinde.

[I. II. 65]

They appear, too, in the baiting of Polonius, in the exchanges with Rosencrantz and Guildenstern, in the nunnery scene with Ophelia. It should be remarked that they also manifest themselves on those occasions, in the soliloquies, when we overhear him communing with himself.

What's *Hecuba* to him, or he to *Hecuba*
That he should weepe for her.

[II. II. 552-3]

To sleepe, perchance to Dreame; I, there's the rub.

[III. I. 65]

The cast of his mind is completely permeated by irony and wryness. What, in fact, is the source of this?

A man is often given to wryness and to the use of irony when he
realises that the posture he is forced to take up relative to an event
and to other people is not one that he would choose himself.
There is a touching and disturbing example of this, as it applies to
Hamlet, at the outset of the play. When he has reflected upon the
words and the injunctions of the Ghost, he cries,

> The time is out of joynt: Oh cursed spite
> That ever I was borne to set it right.
> [I. v. 189–90]

These words are all the more telling coming as they do at the end
of the scene, after the hot words that he has used in saying that he
will avenge his father's death. He sees now that the times have
become disordered, but he equally regrets that it is he who has
been enjoined to restore them to order. We get a strong impression that his regret is the result of his knowledge that he is the
wrong man to set them right. This impression is underlined by the
way in which, as has been noted, he decides to "put on" an antic
disposition. All his decisions to put the disordered time right are,
surely, out of phase with what is required. He should "sweep to his
revenge", but he cannot; he should confront his uncle, but he
does not; he should make his intentions clear to Ophelia, but he
does not; he reflects so keenly that even Horatio, at the graveside,
impatiently says that his inquiries are "too close". While we
experience the play in performance we do not find that one of the
traditional answers to this way of going about things—that is, to
imply that since he is not sure of the Ghost's validity he must be
cautious—is entirely satisfactory. It is unsatisfactory simply
because on Claudius's own testimony we know the Ghost to be
telling the truth.

> Oh my offence is ranke, it smells to heaven
> It hath the primall eldest curse upon't,
> A Brothers murther.
> [III. III. 36–8]

And indeed, if Hamlet suspects the Ghost on one score—the murder—why then does he believe it so easily on the other—the "crime" committed by Gertrude in marrying Claudius? It is quite remarkable that Hamlet reacts much more credulously to what the Ghost confirms about Hamlet's mother (that she has lustfully conjoined with a murderer) than to what the Ghost relates about the fact of the murder. It is equally remarkable that whereas his attitude towards the murderer is sardonic, never seeming to threaten more than verbal taunt, his attitude towards his mother, especially in the closet scene, is full of a dangerous passion.

It is at this point that the posture which the Ghost has tried to force Hamlet into begins to look at odds with the posture that Hamlet, since he has to take some kind of action, wishes to assume—what is wished upon him, and what is desired by him, are at variance. Even before we are witnesses of Hamlet's first meeting with his father's Ghost we have a clear indication of the manner in which he has responded to his father's death. He is in a state of acute melancholy—to the extent of reflecting upon suicide—about what has happened. Yet, it is noticeable that what has darkened his mind seems less the fact of the loss of a dear father than the precipitancy of his mother's marriage, and all that it implies about the slimness of her fidelity. He is expressly outraged by what his mother has done.

> . . . Frailty, thy name is woman.
> A little Month, or ere those shooes were old,
> With which she followed my poore Fathers body
> Like *Niobe*, all teares Why she, even she
> (O Heaven! a beast that wants discourse of Reason
> Would have mourn'd longer) married with mine unkle,
> My Fathers Brother.
>
> [I. II. 146-52)

Hamlet is called upon to avenge the wrong deed. The Ghost wishes him to leave his mother to heaven, and reminds him in the closet scene that his "true purpose" (the avenging of his father's death upon Claudius) is almost blunted. The Ghost has cast Hamlet in the role of avenging angel, when all his faculties cry out for him to be a moral scourge. The Ghost has asked him to be active, but his disposition is to be reflective, intellectually questioning, and, in moral terms, admonitory. All Hamlet's soliloquies point to this, but one in particular, the most searing in the directness of its meaning and the effect of its language, describes the torturing irony which inhabits the soul of this man called up to be one thing but, by disposition, capable of being only another. In the "rogue and peasant slave" soliloquy, the overall effect is that two Hamlets are confronting one another. The actor-prince most certainly now has a dual role. The reflective man and the unwilling man of action confront one another. The resulting contrasts are stark in their dramatic effect.

> Yet I,
> A dull and muddy-metled Rascall, peake
> Like John a-dreames, unpregnant of my cause,
> And can say nothing.
>
> [II. II. 560–3]

And, what, in the end, is the result of this drama in which Hamlet faces himself upon the stage of his own sensibilities? It is a decision of superb, and at the same time, pathetic compromise. He will not be merely reflective, nor merely active. He will concoct yet another drama wherein "the conscience of the King" will be caught. He retreats, yet again, into his disposition not to come to full terms with the reality of the situation, but to push it into the realms of histrionic illusion. His reason, as always, seems subtle and logical enough. He has heard "that guilty creatures sitting at a play" will be so conscience-stricken by what they witness that they will reveal their guilt. Yet we are not convinced that this tells the whole truth. We are more convinced of two unspoken things. First, that it is a half-hearted, half-cocked motivation and, second, that the plan suits his disposition more than it seems likely to minister to the avowed intention of revealing Claudius's guilt. Hamlet's delight that the mouse-trap play does, in fact, prise out from Claudius a guilty reaction is the delight of a man who un-expectedly finds that his plan has worked, rather than of one whose suspicions have now been proved.

It has already been noted that Hamlet's arguments for not killing Claudius at prayers are both subtle and logical—too subtle, in fact, considering the enormity of Claudius's deed and the virtual certainty that Hamlet now possesses of his guilt. Yet he holds back his sword—his heart does not seem to lie in its blade. He is almost cool in his reflectiveness as he speaks behind the back of the unsuspecting Claudius.

> Now might I do it pat, now he is praying,
> And now Ile doo't, and so he goes to Heaven,
> And so am I reveng'd: that would be scann'd,
> A Villaine kills my Father, and for that
> I his foule Sonne, do this same Villaine send
> To heaven.
>
> [III. III. 73–7]

Yet, if we compare this with the temperature of his language when he speaks to his mother, the proposition that he had been called upon to avenge, for him, the wrong deed, begins to acquire confirmation. He is so fiercely outraged by his mother because her deeds offend his intense moral susceptibilities—but in a very particular way. He feels himself to be a tainted wether of the flock. The kind of self-indulgence which feeds Hamlet's histrionic temperament is also present in the conclusions that his mind makes from his reflections on his mother's crime. She has not merely stained herself, but has stained Hamlet.

One of the most prevalent explanations of Hamlet's wildness of behaviour and words to Ophelia is that they are an example of the extent to which his mind has become unbalanced. In fact, if we accept the explanation that he himself feels tainted by his mother's deed, his words and actions to Ophelia have a poignant logic about them and, moreover, his rejection of her makes sense—a strained, nervous sense assuredly, but nevertheless one not dissociated from a clear theme. The truth of the paradox he speaks to her (which, let it be noted, he himself recognises as a paradox) is proven, for him, in the ironic words which end the "paradox"—"now the time gives it proofe".

> . . . the power of Beautie, will sooner transforme Honestie
> from what it is, to a Bawd, then the force of Honestie can
> translate Beauty into his likenesse. This was sometimes
> a Paradox, but now the time gives it proofe.
>
> [III. I. 111–15]

The words are a reference to the "dishonesty" in which his mother
has involved herself. His next words are of great importance and
recall us, directly, to the concept that he feels tainted by his
mother's action.

> For vertue cannot so innoculate our old stocke but
> We shall rellish of it.
>
> [III. I. 118–19]

The implication of this remark, in the context of Hamlet's feeling
of having been tainted by his mother's deed, is amplified consider-
ably when we put it against the accusations that he later hurls at
her in the closet scene. He will show her, he says, her "inmost
heart". When he asks if it is the king who has slumped dead
behind the arras after his blind sword has pierced it, he cries,

> A bloody deed—almost as bad good Mother,
> As Kill a King, and marrie with his Brother.
>
> [III. IV. 28–9]

He promises that he will "wring her heart". When he compares
the portrait of his father with that of Claudius he does not dwell
upon the horror of murder, but on the superiority of the one to the
other. He proceeds to draw the conclusions from the contrast
between the two pictures—it amounts to a passionate, morally
outraged, condemnation of Gertrude's crime in marrying
Claudius. Her act "blurs the grace of blush and modesty", it takes
away the rose from "the fair forehead of an innocent love";
the act has made "marriage-vows as false as dicers' oaths". In
all, it seems to him an act of "rank corruption" which "infects
unseen".

Melodramatically as all this is expressed, with Hamlet's typical
acting-out in his words of the nature of deeds and thoughts, the

moral indignation (so detailed in its evidence) seems to come from some deep source in Hamlet himself. The meaning of his previous words to Ophelia begins to take on an importance in terms of the nature of his moral indignation, and of his behaviour to Ophelia. No virtue, he says, is capable of cancelling out the taint with which his mother's deed has infected his "stock"—that is, his blood and lineage. His cruel assault on Ophelia's emotions, therefore, has the aspect both of a kind of protection of her, and a condemnation of himself. She is to get to a nunnery lest she be "a breeder of sinners" (got by Hamlet himself upon her). He could, he says, accuse himself of such things "that it were better my mother had not borne me". He rationalises what his faults are—pride, revengefulness, ambition; he pictures himself an arrant knave "crawling between earth and heaven", but these rationalisations hardly explain the anguish with which he tries to dismiss Ophelia from his heart. His manner of protecting her against herself, who would be a breeder of sinners, shows the extent to which his mother's crime has infected his moral and emotional susceptibilities. In the nunnery scene, one of the most pitiful elements is the way in which his fierce and implied protectiveness of the single female shades into outright condemnation of the whole female sex. Gertrude has outraged womanhood; she has tarnished and corrupted its image and its reality. To this extent all womanhood (including Ophelia) has become as one foul and objectionable thing.

All this, Ophelia does not know and if she did would not, we are assured, understand. She responds, one may say, conventionally —though certainly not without deep shock. She remembers the Hamlet that was—renowned as courtier, soldier, scholar, man of fashion—and grieves, like any affronted and jilted girl, at the loss of her dear lover.

One of the most poignant elements in the tragedy of Hamlet is that his moral susceptibilities, kindled into fierce hate by the deeds of one woman, cancel, by their heat, his desire to love another woman. He can only express his love for Ophelia when she is dead (then, she is beyond the need for his curiously self-abnegating kind of protection) and is shrived by death of her connection with the tainted image of womanhood that his mother has created for him.

> I lov'd *Ophelia*: fortie thousand Brothers
> Could not (with all their quantitie of Love)
> Make up my summe.
>
> [v. i. 263–4]

The offence of his mother is against the order of love and all its tenets. It is this which Hamlet wants to avenge by "cleansing" like Jaques the "foul body of the infected world". But Hamlet is pacific by nature, because he is so much governed by his high conception of the order and validity of love. For him to kill would be to be guilty of an offence against his nature and against the spirit of love as he so deviously expresses it. The fact that love, in terms of order, fidelity, honesty, truth and indeed beauty (witness his description of his father) is an all-enveloping and governing element in his personality, is evidenced by the fact that the offence that has been committed against it by Gertrude has (even before the Ghost's revelations) taken away from him any zest for life itself. It is as if the heart has been taken out of his universe. A sense of the corruption of life stains his thoughts and his words, and what we may take to be a former apprehension of life's purpose, beauty and order, exists now as a kind of nostalgia. B. Ifor Evans[10] makes this point in another way, but one which underlines, very forcibly, the cast of Hamlet's mind:

> We have in Hamlet a mind that strikes out to undiscovered
> beauties, and then, by some complex anatomising of
> experience, destroys the beauty he has created. "Why", he
> asked Horatio, "may not imagination trace the noble dust of
> Alexander, till he find it stopping a bung-hole?" Horatio
> answered with a comment that might apply to a number of
> Hamlet's speculations: "Twere to consider too curiously, to
> consider so."

The "case" of Hamlet, then, is that of a perfectionist in thought and feeling, subjected to the most severe undermining of the very thing which is the object of his sense of perfection—the spirit and truth of ordered love. The wryness and irony of so much of his tone of address, which has been mentioned, is a kind of emblem of the "fractured and corroborate" state of his mind and feelings now that they have been bereft of that which made life meaningful for him—the belief in the efficacy of love. Beneath his wryness and irony, his cynicism and despair, can be glimpsed, time and time again, vestiges of what he has lost. In so many of his dealings with people—with Ophelia, with his mother, with Polonius, with Horatio, with Laertes, with the players—what we sense is either deep love, or affection, or those qualities overborne by a cynicism which circumstances have forced upon him. He is, to repeat, asked to kill when what he wants to do is to heal.

Hamlet's religion is, in a way, the religion of love; when that is shaken, he is unable to find any reason for not being aweary of the world. His involvement in his religion is complete. Love as friendship he worships in Horatio, but he finds its negative in Rosencrantz and Guildenstern. Love as something which finds its ultimate expression in true marriage he has witnessed in the union of his father and mother, but he has found its negative in that of Gertrude and Claudius. Love, catching him in its nearest way, as that which binds men and women together, he has found in Ophelia, but once his "religious" faith is shattered, he cannot, with her, or with anybody, go through the motions of worship.

The critical procedure by which the play of *Hamlet* is regarded as the first of a group of "tragedies" marked off in theme and tone from what has gone before, ignores or underestimates the "one-ness" of Shakespeare's mind and imagination. *Hamlet* is less the first of a group of plays which seem to set an entirely new course in his imaginative world, than the first most profound exploration of a theme which had become a unifying spirit of all his plays by 1598–1599. *Twelfth Night, As You Like It, Measure for Measure, Troilus and Cressida,* in particular, are concerned with various aspects of love. They are, in series, an exploration of the theme which encompasses romantic affirmation and cynical doubt. The "tragedies" take the exploration of love much further, but it still remains a unifying spirit of the plays. In *Hamlet* love as the ulti-mate exemplar of fidelity, honesty and human kindness is the

obsession of the protagonist; in *Othello*, love as the victim of
stupidity, rancour and jealousy is the burden of the play; in
King Lear, love betrayed by cupidity, filial ingratitude and mulish
pride is the dominating theme; in *Macbeth*, love in the shape of
duty, honour, is the victim of ambition.

Shakespeare thus moves through myriad aspects of the concept
of love—from its more obvious and pleasing manifestations in the
romantic coupling of man and woman to profound examinations
of the disorder, grief and tragedy that ensue when love is despoiled.

It is not easy to prevent any discussion of the play of *Hamlet*
becoming an obsession with the protagonist at the expense of the
other characters. Yet perhaps the instinct to concentrate almost
exclusively upon him has some objective justification. There is no
other play of Shakespeare's where the minor characters so
definitely subserve the presence of the protagonist. We find ourselves obliged to consider Polonius, Gertrude, Claudius, Ophelia,
only to find, time and time again, that they hardly exist except in
terms of Hamlet himself. They are "partial" characters in a sense
which is far from true of, for example, Gloucester, Regan,
Goneril, and Iago.

It is only because Polonius is accidentally killed by Hamlet that
we have cause to consider his position in the play; it is only because
Gertrude is Hamlet's mother that we regard her; it is only because
Claudius is Hamlet's uncle and also his intended victim that he is
important; it is only because of Hamlet's communication of the
nature of his relationship with her that Ophelia enters into our sensibilities. The truth is that, so comparatively under-developed are
they as characters, they occasion that kind of puzzled questioning
which has, for so long, attached itself to critical comment on
Hamlet himself. Is Polonius a mere old fool, or has he more shrewd-
ness than folly? Was Gertrude a willing and active partner to
actual murder or is she a simple, over-sexed, unintelligent
woman? How "innocent" is Ophelia? How "evil" is Claudius?
These are questions which arise at every reading of the text and,
significantly, at performances of the play. Polonius has been
played as grave elderly statesman, stumping along the final corri-

dors of power, and he has, with equal success, been depicted as a senile comic. Gertrude has been played as a gorgeous, sexually alive, dark beauty and, with equal success, as a bewildered pawn in power politics. Ophelia has been played as a sexy miss (revealing in her "mad" scenes the bawdy configurations of her sub-conscious), and as fragile innocent hammered into madness by grief for her father and for the loss of Hamlet's love. Claudius has been played as rhodomontade villain, vicious, dangerous, but, with equal success, he has been depicted as a man of intellectual and moral sensitivity, suffering pangs of conscience for the deed which was an inexplicable aberration in an otherwise noble man.

The text does give some scope for such variations simply because these characters are not fully developed in their own right. Nevertheless, it is a remarkable fact that each one of them is given one scene in the play in which each is, if only for a short time, "built up" beyond the creative generalisations in which each is largely conceived. Polonius's precepts to Laertes; Gertrude's reactions in the closet scene; Ophelia's "mad" scene; Claudius's "prayer" scene—these scenes give body to characters who, on the whole, lack substance. The significant feature of the scenes is that, in their different ways, they allow the characters to come closer to our sympathies and to our understanding.

If Polonius is made to look foolish in his scenes with Hamlet and in his tautological encounters with Claudius, the speeches to Laertes—full of saws as they are, long-windedly as they are expressed—bespeak a caring man, and a man who, though the practice of virtue has ossified into theorising, has principles and has known the world shrewdly. If we tend, overall, to be impatient of Polonius, this scene tempers our impatience. He is a well-meaning old man in whom tautological speculation has replaced shrewd practice, but he has retained feeling and a sense of duty and has much love in him.

Again, if we are led, overall, to see Gertrude merely as an unthinking loose woman, driven by expediency and sexual appetite, we have to modify this simple reaction when we witness her pitiful demonstration of half-realised conscience, fear and bewildered affection in the closet scene. If we are disposed, at first, to see

Ophelia as a mere pathetic victim of circumstances, we are forced to reach deeper into our sympathies when we contemplate, in the "mad" scenes, the extent to which her mind and heart have been broken. Up to this point she is a victim of circumstance but, upon her madness, we realise what the word "victim" means—she ceases, for a short time, to be a cog in the plot machine, and becomes a deeply suffering, deeply affecting human being.

Claudius shows few signs of being more than a nervous autocrat until we witness him at prayer. It is in this scene that we learn that any simple decision about the nature of this man is misplaced. He is pulled out of the status of secondary villain in a revenge play and placed in a more credible light.

These four episodes, while they have the effect of subtilising the characters and drawing them nearer to our sympathies, have another important role in our experience of the play. They help us to realise, despite the concentration by Shakespeare on Hamlet's viewpoint of the world of Elsinore, that this world exists independently and has its own tensions and realities. At certain points, well distributed throughout the play, it is as if we suddenly leave the immense chambers of Hamlet's own mind and find ourselves standing, with the rest, in an uneasy society, all of whose inhabitants are in a state of apprehension.

Apprehension is indeed the keynote of the society of Elsinore. It does not seem so much corrupt as gripped by a force which it is unable to contend with or even fully understand—that force is the presence of Hamlet. Yet, if it is an apprehensive society, it is also one which is essentially political in the manner in which it responds to circumstances. One of the most skilful features of Shakespeare's handling of his plot is the manner in which the events, and particularly Hamlet's responses to them, are "naturalised". Without the shrewd pointing of the political nature of the responses of so many of the major elements of the court, the play would be in danger of seeming to be a profoundly poetic demonstration of an unusual man's over-exaggerated point of view.

We have a sense, certain if not strong, of the existence of faction in this court. Horatio *does* seem to belong to a faction which, at the least, disapproves of Claudius's accession. We have a glimpse of the reasons why Polonius is so privy to the king's ear; he has, we instinctively believe, been instrumental in ensuring Claudius's election to the throne.

> Assure, you my good Liege,
> I hold my dutie, as I hold my Soule,
> Both to my God, one to my gracious King.
> [II. II. 43-5]

We are given a powerful demonstration of the force of autocratic intrigue, and the way in which the political minion will cleave to the seat of power, in the episodes involving Rosencrantz and Guildenstern.

We watch with unsurprised amusement the political diletante and sycophant Osric—on the first rungs of a ladder of service which perhaps, years before, Polonius had stepped on his way to the most privy rooms of state secret and intrigue.

Above all, the "naturalising" of the play by examples of political action and thought is achieved by the presence of Fortinbras. We feel, immediately, the broadening out of the context of the play's action. He comes, shining, from a world elsewhere than Elsinore, but he, like the rest of them, is a political man come to establish his politically conceived rights.

It is these things which make Elsinore "real" and, at the same time, increase the tragic loneliness of Hamlet himself. Although he mentions his succession and election, Shakespeare never puts so much emphasis upon this as to make us think that Hamlet is, like the rest, a political man. He remains an outcast, an outraged artist, finding, as Shaw says, "the duties dictated by conventional revenge as disagreeable a burden as commerce is to a poet." Shaw, in reviewing Forbes Robertson's Hamlet at the Lyceum in 1897,[11] said:

> Mr Forbes Robertson is essentially a classical actor. . . .
> What I mean by classical is that he can present a dramatic
> hero as a man whose passions are those which have produced
> the philosophy, the poetry, the art, and the statecraft of the
> world, and not merely those which have produced its
> weddings, coroners' inquests and executions. And that is
> just the sort of actor that Hamlet requires.

Shaw had perceived what a few great actors have perceived—
that the tragedy of Hamlet the Dane is that of an artist called
upon to execute the work of an artisan.

Othello

Othello is built on a much more ordinary human scale than any of
the other tragic heroes. It is partly for this reason that the play
itself has held a particular popularity for theatre audiences. Its
attraction can also be attributed to the insistent "domesticity" of
its plot and theme. It is the one tragedy which comes very near
inducing the possibility in the audience of their feeling—"There
but for the grace of God, go I." It concerns itself with love, hate,
deceit, treachery, brutality, affection, duty, as do the other
tragedies, but here, they are scaled down to familiar proportions.
The kind of marital jealousy shown by Othello we recognise
immediately—sometimes with a shock—as a very close reflection
of what we may have seen or heard about in actual experience.
The kind of "accidents" by which Othello is duped are almost
ludicrously obvious in the manner in which they dictate the actual
plot-line; yet the very disproportion between their petty nature
and the terrible tragedy which they trigger off, makes the play
seem agonisingly "true" to what we call real life. Iago, alone,
seems not to fit exactly in with the recognisable and familiar
realism of the characters of the play. It is true that we catch sharp
glimpses in him of a kind of reasonless envy, malice and duplicity,
which make us realise, with a start, that we have known men like
this; at the same time so enormous is the build up of hate, so
puzzling is the question of motivation, that he seems to stand
apart, to a large measure, from the mode of the rest of the
characters.

   Why Shakespeare should have turned to write a play in which a
Moor is the protagonist is not known. He continually surprises
with the manner in which he grasps firmly at stories and source
plots, which are in themselves unremarkable but, for him, are
most valuable ore. In this case he found the story in Cinthio's
Hecatommithi.[12] This book is divided into ten decades, each one

dealing with a different subject. The seventh novel in the book begins:

> There once lived in Venice a Moor, who was very valiant and of a handsome person; and having given proofs in war of great skill and prudence, he was highly esteemed by the Signoria of the Republic, who in rewarding deeds of valour advanced the interests of the state.[13]

Perhaps, indeed, Shakespeare was intrigued by the possibilities of what could be done with three such sharply distinguished characters as are described by Cinthio:

> A Moor, who was very valiant and of a handsome person .... he was highly esteemed by the Signoria of the republic.

> A virtuous lady of marvelous beauty named Disdemona fell in love with the Moor.

> Amongst the soldiery there was an ensign, a man of handsome figure, but of the most depraved nature in the world.

Shakespeare's play moves very strictly within the boundaries of this triangle. There is no highly developed sub-plot; the destinies of everyone are held closely within the triangle. Yet, although the play is architecturally neat, and though it is the most insistently domestic of the great tragedies, it poses a number of questions, few of which do not involve us in some subjective decisions. "What motivates Iago?" "How innocent is Desdemona?" "Are the 'accidents' of the plot too obtrusive, and do they, in fact, rob the play of that relentless inevitability which characterises the other tragedies?" "What part is Othello's colour meant to play in the development of the plot and theme?"

This last question, is, for the contemporary audience, the most intriguing of all. It involves all the susceptibilities and prejudices about colour which have forced their way into humanity's consciousness in the last few decades of this century. It is a truism to state that the depth and variety of both our emotional and intellectual preoccupation with the "problem" of colour were unknown in Shakespeare's time, yet it is worth emphasising now that modern directors are so obsessed with the principle of making Shakespeare's plays vital for the twentieth century, that there is a danger that specifically twentieth-century notions about colour are likely to be grafted on to Othello. This is not to say that the play has nothing, of itself, to say to us about "colour", yet we must be clear what it does, in fact, declare, and what it does not. O. J. Campbell has a timely warning on this matter:

> In present-day North America a Negro Othello is likely to pervert the meaning that Shakespeare gave the situation, to twist it into a problem of miscegenation . . . this is disastrous to a correct interpretation of the action, for Othello is no struggler up from slavery for status, but an aristocrat who fetches his "life and being" from "men of royal siege".[14]

Campbell's words are the more to be regarded in the light of the contradictory and emotionally expressed conceptions of Othello that have appeared in critical works throughout the nineteenth and the twentieth centuries. The complications of the problem may be indicated by two nineteenth-century remarks. The first is by Mary Preston, an American critic:

> Shakespeare was too correct a delineator of human nature to have coloured Othello *black*, if he had personally acquainted himself with the idiosyncracies of the African race. . . . *Othello* was a *white man*![15]

The second by G. H. Lewes:

> Othello is black—the very tragedy lies there.[16]

It is unlikely that Shakespeare would have had close contact with the Moorish race from which, he is careful to emphasise, Othello came. On the other hand it is more than possible that he had seen and met with Moorish ambassadors or seamen. What he is very aware of is the close relationship between Venice and the Moors. They traded with Venice, and their mercenary warriors had fought both with and against the Venetians. They were a proud, martial

and civilised race; the rich blood of their stock is well described by
Henry Reed:

> [Othello] was one of that adventurous race of men who,
> striking out from the heart of Arabia, had made conquest of
> Persia and Syria; and, overturning the ancient sovereignty of
> Egypt, swept in victory along the whole Northern coast of
> Africa; and, passing thence across the narrow Frith of the
> Mediterranean, scattered the dynasty of the Goths with
> Roderic at their head . . . how true to his nature was it for
> Othello to stand in conscious pride—the descendants of a
> race of kings, the representative of the Arabs who had been
> sovereigns of Europe—his spirit glowing with noble
> ancestral memories; and, on the other hand, how perfectly
> consistent it was with the debasing malignity of Iago, and
> with the petulant disappointment of Roderigo, to be blind
> to all that ennobled and dignified the Moorish name.[17]

This, then, is the basis of Othello's character, pride of race, martial
courage, with centuries of civilised achievement as well as fierce
barbarism behind him. Yet, he is also black, and it is well to
examine, in general terms, what kind of "placement" his colour
and race has in the play. There are three main effects. First, his
colour as "the cause" is referred to; second, his general appearance
and bearing, in consort with the life he has led and his place of
birth, constitute an exciting mystery for Desdemona—for her he is
excitingly "different". Certainly his colour does play some part in
Brabantio's outraged condemnation of Othello's marriage with
Desdemona. The word "black" is mentioned several times and is
used by Othello himself when he speculates as to why Desdemona
has been unfaithful to him. There can be little doubt that an association is made, by Othello's enemies, between his colour and
what they take to be his vices. Iago makes the most violent association when he goads Brabantio with what has happened to his
daughter:

> Even now, now, very now, an old blacke Ram
> Is tupping your white Ewe.
>
> [I. i. 89–90]

Yet, Othello occupies high status; he is well regarded by many people; he is trusted by the state to important office. Othello does not live, we may say, in a racialist society which would deny him the opportunity for advancement. He is not a pariah; he is debarred from nothing that any white man would accept as a natural right. On the contrary, in the context of the society of Venice, Othello takes precedence over many eminent white people. "Colour" then is most definitely not an issue, in this play, in the sense in which it has become an issue in modern society and in many examples of modern literature. The three most specific attitudes towards Othello in this play are those of Iago, Brabantio and Desdemona. For each one of them "colour" plays some part, but it is peripheral as compared to the part it plays in the consciousness of the twentieth century.

Iago uses "colour" only as an additive to a hatred whose real source lies elsewhere. It is not the main issue for him. He does not despise Othello because he is black, but the fact of his blackness may be said to be an additional reason for disliking him. Brabantio's affronted fury leaps to its height when he thinks of the black ram tupping his ewe, but it is very significant that the accusation that he hurls at Othello is that he has used "magic" to ensnare Desdemona. For Brabantio, Othello is a dangerous stranger he does not understand; he has come, with pride and status, from some dim exotic land where mesmeric arts are practised. Desdemona's expression of love for Othello and, importantly, her explanation of how she grew to love him, is based (in a somewhat childlike way) upon the appeal of mystery— the fairy prince, from places unimaginable, has come to life for her. It is curiously ironic that Desdemona loves Othello for the very reason that Brabantio rejects him. They both see him as the mysterious stranger but with completely opposed results.

Othello is therefore no more reviled simply because he is black than he is respected because he is black. He is an exotic stranger, an outsider in the world of Venice. For those who love him or can appreciate his qualities and his value to them he is a welcome outsider—a saviour to the hierarchy of Venice, a fairy prince to Desdemona. For those who hate him he is an outsider, but in the sense of one that is to be reviled, either for some real or imagined vice (to suit Iago's purposes) or for his utter difference from an accepted and familiar social norm (to Brabantio). To the former he is a "lascivious Moor", a "Barbary horse"; to the latter he is one who has "enchanted" Desdemona, bound her "in chains of magic" and used "foul charms"; he is "a practiser of arts inhibited".

The first speech of consequence that Othello makes seems to emphasise the strangeness of the man. We catch glimpses of a life led in far places, in stern circumstances. When the Duke gives him permission to tell of his wooing of Desdemona, the outlines of that life are filled in with exotic and romantic colourings. He has had "hair-breadth scapes", wandered in "deserts idle", and has met

> The *Antropophague*, and men whose heads
> Doe grow beneath their shoulders.
>
> [I. III. 144–5]

Moreover, he has, from the age of seven, led the hard life of a soldier—from childhood he has wandered with rough, harsh assembly. Desdemona has grown to love him for he is an unusual man, and because she pities the sufferings of his youth. What Othello tells us in his speech is the story of a romantic girl who has found her dreams and imagination realised, and of a man who has unexpectedly found beauty, worship and pity. This is the basis of their love—the romantic innocent child and the experienced man have each had a dream realised.

The passionate extent, the blind fury of Othello's jealousy, is explicable entirely within the context of these two factors—the first, the "outsider" position of Othello, the second, the unexpected realisation of a dream. This tragedy is the result of the wilful and clever increasing of Othello's sense of being an outsider and a deliberate destruction of his belief that his dream of love, fidelity and beauty has been realised in Desdemona. It cannot be over-emphasised that behind all that Othello says of Desdemona up to the point where Iago's jealousy begins to work its poison, there is a note of joyous surprise that he has won her. It expresses itself in his pride in her as his wife; it lurks in his description of how

she reacted to his stories; it comes to the surface in his greeting to
her at Cyprus:

> It gives me wonder great, as my content
> To see you heere before me. Oh my Soules Joy.
> [II. I. 181–2]

And he adds,

> For I feare,
> My Soule hath her content so absolute
> That not another comfort like to this
> Succeeds in unknowne Fate.
> [II. I. 188–91]

And, as if joy is bursting his heart, he cries,

> I cannot speak enough of this content;
> It stoppes me heere; it is too much of joy.
> [II. I. 194–5]

Criticism of the kind which sees Othello as a blind dupe from
whom a thin veneer of civilised behaviour is easily removed, does
not take sufficient note of what Desdemona means to him. He has
discovered something in her he never before possessed; a beautiful
woman has overlooked men of her own clime and come to love
him. When he says that it is "too much of joy" it is almost literally
true—he never imagined that reality could fulfil desire, hope,
imagination, in this way.

   This man whose dreams have come to life is opposed by one
who is a conscious artist in villainy. Like Richard III, Iago has been
designated, by critics, as a form of medieval Vice; yet, as with
Richard III, this description does not seem, in the closest analysis,
to give more than a general framework to something that is more
subtle and complex. Iago is, like Richard (and like the Vice), an
emblem of evil, but, like Richard, there is a quality in him which
goes beyond the merely allegorical. The Vice in medieval drama
manifested evil in as definite a manner as an angel manifested
good. When drama was a fixed ritual, ministering to stated and
accepted beliefs, its constituent parts—plot, theme, language and

character—had, to a large extent, a symbolic value. The plot stood for a known series of events, the theme bespoke and underlined the meaning of those events, the language memorialised conditioned reflexes of response, the characters pictorialised in action a natural equation—on one side stood the plus of good, on the other the minus of evil. There was no cross-over. On the minus side the vice worked.

The heirs of this stock theatrical representation of evil are abundant in Elizabethan drama, including Shakespeare's. There can be little doubt that Iago himself is made up of the basic ingredients of the Vice figure. He is completely amoral; he patently enjoys being and doing evil; his "reasons" for committing wrong are unconvincing. He seems to acquire motive from some dark evil force of which he is an earthly agent; he is mentally agile in his pursuit of wrong-doing; he is a master of deception. Such characteristics, typical of the Vice, lie, too, in different degrees of intensity within Richard III. To an extent such characters, for an Elizabethan audience, would have been accepted as stock "props" in any play where evil was pitted against good in an intent fashion. Yet neither Richard, nor Iago are simply this. Shakespeare, typically, builds upon traditional and conventional material, and all his "Vice" characters are given the additional dimension of seeming actual. There is always much in them that is only too human while, at the same time, we are kept aware of dark affiliations they have with the supernatural. Kenneth Muir quotes Bernard Spivack on this conjunction. He describes it as:

> The seam between the drama of allegory and the drama of nature, as well as between the kind of motivations proper to each.[18]

Muir adds:

> In other words, Iago is both a stage devil, deriving ultimately from the Vice of the Morality plays, and a character in a more sophisticated Elizabethan tragedy. He hates goodness, at the same time as he has psychological motives for hating Othello.[19]

These "psychological motives" are difficult to credit yet, para-doxically, they give this particular tragedy an awful patina of reality. None of the reasons given by Iago are ever proven, yet they might be true. Even more important, though we find them difficult to believe, we recognise their mode and manner of expression as only too typical of the processes by which envious, rancorous and dangerous men serve their own ends.

This play exerts a unique fascination. In no other of his plays does Shakespeare concentrate so much upon the minutiae of a relationship between two men. Yet it is a relationship of an unusual and terrible kind. It is based entirely upon duplicity; it is a most terrible demonstration of the difference between what is and what seems. Iago, with the most slender resources of evidence, and dangerously near being unmasked at every stage, mounts an offensive of tremendous ferocity and audacity. The various stages of the offensive, the deployment of weapons, are shown with remarkable dramatic skill.

The reasons given by Iago, at different points in the play, for his hatred of Othello are firstly, that Cassio has been appointed lieutenant instead of himself; secondly, that it is "thought abroad" that Othello has had sexual relations with Emilia; thirdly, that Cassio has also had relations with Emilia; fourthly, that he wants Desdemona himself. He also mentions that Michael Cassio

> Hath a dayly beauty in his life
> That makes me ugly.
> [v. i. 19–20]

There are three themes running through these "reasons". They are envy, sexual jealousy and self-regard. Of these three, the last is the most persistently expressed; indeed the other two become subservient to the immense self-regard as the play proceeds. At the very beginning he tells Roderigo, "I know my price, I am worth no worse a place." His every soliloquy implies a fear that he is not being regarded in the way he should be. The extent to which even sexual jealousy is subservient to his self-regard is clearly shown in his references to his own wife's alleged infidelity with Othello. In Act One, scene three, he says,

> I hate the Moore,
> And it is thought abroad that 'twixt my sheets
> He ha's done my Office. I know not if't be true,
> But I, for meere suspition in that kinde,
> Will do, as if for Surety.

[I. III. 380-4]

Later on in Act Two, scene one, he says,

> For that I do suspect the lustie Moore
> Hath leap'd into my seat. The thought whereof
> Doth (like a poysonous Minerall) gnawe my inwardes.

[II. I. 289-91]

As Kenneth Muir says,

> Iago however, is not so much concerned with Emilia's
> unfaithfulness, as with the fact that he is despised or pitied,
> or an object of ridicule as a cuckold; and this is intolerable
> to his self-esteem.[20]

It is noticeable how the word "I" runs with repetitive frequency
through Iago's soliloquies and noticeable too how, like Richard
III, part of his self-regard has a kind of chuckling celebration of his
own cleverness and duplicity.

> How am I then a Villaine
> To Counsell *Cassio* to this paralell course,
> Directly to his good? Divinitie of hell,
> When divels will the blackest sinnes put on,
> They do suggest at first with heavenly shewes
> As I do now.

[II. III. 337-42]

Even at the very end when all his villainy is revealed he preserves
a kind of mocking self-assurance, a determination to assert the
immense self-conceit of "I am what I am". When Othello stabs
him, he cries,

> I bleed Sir, but not kill'd.

[V. II. 292]

His last words are,

> Demand me nothing: what you know, you know:
> From this time forth, I never will speake word.
>
> [v. ii. 306–7]

We have to see all his alleged "reasons", and indeed his machina-
tions against Othello within the matrix of this self-regard. If no
"reasons" were ever given or implied, it would still be enough for
us to know that a man of such extraordinary self-conceit would be
likely to find opportunity to display it by wicked deeds.

The process by which he destroys Othello has much in it which,
once again, displays the skill of an actor. It is often forgotten,
especially by those who see Othello as a stupid, blind dupe, that
Iago succeeds in duping everyone. He is, like Richard iii, a consummate actor who can exert his power over the most intelligent,
as well as the most gullible. Michael Cassio trusts him, Desdemona
seems almost to admire his forthrightness, the stupid Roderigo is
mesmerised by him. The basis of the deception he practises on
them all is his studied "putting on" of the face of honesty. Othello
trusts him completely—to him he is simply "honest Iago". It
should be emphasised, in view of the fact that Iago is often held
to be a complete liar, that, in point of fact, his duplicity is subtle.
He uses honesty itself in the service of deception. This is shown
with superb effect in the scene where the tipsy Cassio has wounded
Montano and Othello is seeking the truth. He gets it—from
honest Iago.

His account is absolutely correct. It is so true, so mild in its
expression, so "fair" to Cassio, that Othello immediately suspects
that the honest teller of the circumstances is deliberately playing
down Cassio's part in the brawl.

> I know *Iago*
> Thy honestie, and love doth mince this matter,
> Making it light to *Cassio*.
>
> [ii. iii. 237–9]

Iago has achieved his purpose—by honesty.

He does, in fact, make his attack on Othello not only with the

simple device of lying, but with a subtle usage of calculated
candour. We can believe him, knowing as we do of his self-regard,
when he says,

> Good name in Man, and woman (deere my lord)
> Is the immediate Jewel of their Soules.
>
> [III. III. 159–60]

He does no more than echo Brabantio when he says,

> She did deceive her Father, marrying you.
>
> [III. III. 210]

He confirms what Othello knows when he claims,

> And when she seemed to shake, and feare your lookes,
> She lov'd them most.
>
> [III. III. 211]

He is ironically right in his advice.

> My lord, I would I might intreat your Honor
> To scan this thing no farther: Leave it to time.
>
> [III. III. 248–9]

He is probably telling the truth when he says that he saw Cassio
wiping his beard with the handkerchief that Othello gave to
Desdemona. Even if he did not actually witness the occurrence,
he knows perfectly well that the handkerchief is in Cassio's keep-
ing. It is wrong to assume that Othello's belief in Iago's honesty (or
indeed Cassio's belief) is entirely misplaced. Iago, indeed, is no
simple deceiver—he can wreak havoc and create corruption by a
shrewd exercise of plain speaking.

Yet his use of the lie direct is a mixture of cool calculation and
breath-taking opportunism. A good deal of the play's dramatic
impact on us is, indeed, the result of watching and listening to a
man walking a knife-edge between success and disaster. Some of
his lies are as blandly calculated as his truth-telling. He prides himself upon his patient calculation of his intentions.

> Thou know'st we worke by Wit, and not by Witchcraft
> And Wit depends on dilatory time.
>
> [II. III. 360–1]

and gives several examples of his careful assembly of false evidence. He tells Othello that he does not think it could have been Cassio sneaking "away so guilty-like" from Desdemona's presence. "My lord, you know I love you," spoken right at the moment of the birth of Othello's suspicions, is outright and calculated hypocrisy. Yet, what is most striking about Iago is his use of what might be true, and his audaciously correct reading of the reaction that his evidence will receive. When he says "Ha! I like not that", in order to incite a reaction from Othello to Cassio's meeting with Desdemona, Othello asks "What dost thou say?" He replies "nothing, my lord; or if—I know not what". The onus is thrown upon Othello to consider whether what Iago has said is "nothing" or "something". When he reports Cassio's lascivious behaviour when dreaming, we have no proof that this is a lie, although we are prepared to believe that it is; more to the point is Iago's reply to Othello's "O monstrous! monstrous!" Iago says, "Nay, this was but his dream." There is a terrible and frank reasonableness about it—it could, quite simply, be a truth. This awesomely accurate "placing" of traps, rather than, in most cases, the nature of the traps themselves, constitutes the real evil genius of Iago. He is able to snap up the slightest possibility of placing traps, and to foretell the certain result. Although he has obviously thought of a use for the handkerchief previously, he has no idea that it will fall into his hands at a particular time. When it does, there is a certainty in his knowledge that it will serve his purposes well.

> Trifles light as ayre,
> Are to the jealous, confirmations strong,
> As proofes of holy Writ.
>
> [III. III. 326–8]

There is one further aspect of Iago's superb evil craftsmanship which not only indicates how well he can calculate his victim's reactions, but reminds us of the joy that he takes in his histrionic art. He is able to "pace" the sequence of events which lead to Othello's final breakdown into unredeemable passion. The first "act" of his baiting of Othello he sets at a slow pace; it is composed of offhand remarks, insinuations, affronted dignity. He is in the first stage of playing his line, jerking it slightly, pulling the hook away from his victim, then with a slow swoop advancing it again towards him. This "act" ends with a sudden jerk of direct assault.

> She did deceive her Father, marrying you,
> And when she seem'd to shake, and feare your lookes,
> She lov'd them most.
>
> [III. III. 210–12]

He begins now to increase the pace of his attack, by making more direct statements, and interweaving them with an urgent confidentiality.

> *Iago:* I see this hath a little dash'd your Spirits:
> *Oth:* Not a jot, not a jot.
> *Iago:* Trust me I feare it has.
>   I hope you will consider what is spoke
>   Comes from your Love.
>
> [III. III. 219–21]

The next "act" follows an interval in which he has obtained the handkerchief from Emilia. Now, he is prepared to let Othello have free rein with the passion that has built up in him. Over thirty-seven lines all Iago says is,

> Why, how now, general? No more of that.
> How, now, my lord!
> I am sorry to hear this.
> Is't possible, my lord?
> Is't come to this?
> My noble lord.
>
> [III. III. 339–71]

For the rest, Othello holds the stage and swamps it with his rage, grief and despoiled pride. As the rage begins to abate, Iago comes more into the spotlight, eases the pace a little, then increases it to a

c

terrifying speed with his images of goats and monkeys, his account of Cassio's alleged dream, and then he achieves his supreme climax by kneeling to pledge his service to Othello. Up to this point, Iago has invented, so to say, a play in which passion has risen, abated, then risen again. The final episode of this superbly well-organised drama of passion which Iago is realising, takes on a different tone, pitch and pace. Up to Act Four of the play Iago has used innuendo, truth, half-truth, has played on emotion and passion, but now he becomes explicit; he bursts through Othello's flimsy guard with short staccato thrusts and makes the final cut exactly on the right spot.

> *Iago:* What, to Kisse in private?
> *Oth.:* An unauthoris'd kisse?
> *Iago:* Or to be naked with her Friend in bed,
>   an houre, or more, not meaning any harme?
>
> [IV. I. 2–5]

His trick, by which Othello overhears Cassio seeming to confess to Desdemona's love for him, leads to the final stage of his play. Now, everything he has said to Othello seems to have been proved, and he can afford to give direct and vicious advice.

> Do it not with poyson, strangle her in bed,
> Even the bed she hath contaminated.
> [IV. I. 203–4]

When we contemplate the singular craftsmanship and art of Iago's assault on Othello, and remember the extent to which others have succumbed to it, we have to pause before condemning Othello as a simple gull. The Moor, whose whole life has been dedicated to the raw simplicities of battle, and whose status has come entirely from his prowess and bearing, is subjected to an entirely new experience both in Desdemona's love and in the intellectual subtlety of the way in which that love is destroyed. The Othello whom we see at the beginning of the play is, in Granville Barker's words, "Confident, dignified, candid, calm".[21] He is far from simple-minded. His life has given him the ability to think quickly if not deeply. He is capable of gaining respect by

his qualities of leadership and his palpable honesty. His downfall is
the result of the very pride which he has surrounded himself with
through his marriage to Desdemona. He is as vulnerable as a child
who has had snatched from him the one gift that he has dreamed
about. In a sense the question that is sometimes asked—"Is Desdemona completely guiltless?"—is an irrelevancy. We can never
answer it, so devious is Iago's laying of false evidence. Even more,
it is enough for a man of Othello's quick mind and huge joyous
pride to be suspicious. He asks for proof but even when it is
(apparently) given to him, it seems of less importance to him than
the agony and pain of his personal loss. Time and time again, after
the poison has begun to work, what was surprised and joyous
pride is replaced by the suffering of shattered pride.

> For she had eyes and chose me.
>
> [III. III. 93]

> Shee's gone! I am abus'd.
>
> [III. III. 271]

> Ha! ha! false to me, to me?
>
> [III. 338]

> I had been happy if the general camp,
> Pyoners and all had tasted her sweet body,
> So I had nothing known.
>
> [III. III. 348–50]

> He had my handkerchiefe.
>
> [IV. I. 22]

It is, indeed, the admixture of consuming pride, and apparently
crass gullibility in the man which has occasioned a fairly common
judgement that Othello is of less "status" than the other tragic
heroes. As he plunges into the traps laid by Iago, and as he reveals
more and more of what seems to be selfish pride, we almost forget
the better qualities he revealed at the beginning of the action. In a
sense we learn as an audience, certain positive things from the
other tragic heroes. Hamlet "teaches" us the quality of a noble, if
misguided spirit; Lear's agonies "inform" us of the realities of

great suffering; even Macbeth presents the evidence of the tragedy of fine qualities corrupted. In this specific education which we receive, there is also involved a general realisation of the potential greatness of the human animal. Othello lacks the ability to give us this realisation, and what we learn from him does not seem to have a largeness of import. To learn not to listen to lies, not to believe calumny and place credence upon ridiculously false evidence, seems of less consequence than to apprehend what is given us by Hamlet, Lear and Macbeth.

It may be added, too, that Othello is less intelligent, and of narrower sensibilities, than the others. He does not acquire, with cumulative force, their self-knowledge; although, at the end, he is aware of the crime he has committed, he is more pathetic in his apprehension of it, than profoundly tragic in total realisation. He does not "enlarge" himself in our experience as he falls towards his doom. It is because we can say, of his fall—"There, but for the grace of God, go I", that the protagonist seems smaller than the other three, who take us beyond mere identification.

There is another aspect of the "smallness" of this play when set against the context of the other tragedies. Apart from Iago, no other character or element in the drama intensifies the attendant atmosphere, or implies meanings beyond what is specifically given. Nothing supernatural exists to give the play a dark and brooding hinterland; the sub-plot, dominated by the goofy pretensions of Roderigo, seems miniscule, lacking the pressure on the main plot which, in *Lear* particularly, increases the emotional and psychological weight of the whole; Michael Cassio, Desdemona, Bianca, minister to the plot without imprinting themselves as deeply on our imaginations as do for instance Edgar, Ophelia or Lady Macbeth.

The language of the play too, so indebted to prose, lacks the profound associativeness of the other tragedies. Kenneth Muir says that "Othello's speech cannot be used to undermine his nobility. To most sensitive critics his lines ring true".[22] The fine is—they are only too true. When they reverberate, it is the reverberation of rhetoric which we hear. When they do not, the reader's and the theatregoer's imagination does not take flight—we taxi earth-bound, knowing all the landscape, but unaware of what is beyond the horizon.

Yet, even if its tragic hero is not great, and its own contours are within a limited area, this is still a great play. It is Shakespeare's finest exploration of naturalism. Poetry, in it, is at the service of a present-tense immediacy of effect; character, in it, is held within a matrix of action and experience which, on the whole, is likely to be familiar to an audience. It tells a terrible story with an intensity of concentration upon immediate response by the *dramatis personae*. There is little implied or direct philosophical reflectiveness in them, nor are we incited to reflectiveness by what we witness. Its greatness lies in its stark exposure of the pitiful and pathetically thin line which divides pride from pettiness, truth from falsehood and love from hate. This is a line which, daily, we tread ourselves or see others treading. *Othello* memorialises man's constant and daily vulnerability to his own frailties.

King Lear

The four great tragedies share two general characteristic features. The first is the close domesticity of the initial setting and exposition of the events which will eventually broaden out, both directly and indirectly, to encompass wider horizons and universal human implications. The second is the careful insistence upon the locations of the plays' actions and events. We never allow "A Wood Near Athens" to disabuse us of our certain intuition that it is really a sixteenth-century English wood, peopled by English lovers; we do not allow ourselves to pretend that Kate and Petruchio and Sly have anything but sixteenth-century English blood coursing through their hearts—this Padua is no more than a few leagues from London Bridge. Yet Elsinore, Venice and Cyprus, Dunsinane and Lear's Court remain certainly, either in time or place, far removed from contemporary Elizabethan England. In the tragedies, though their protagonists, their language, the implications of their themes, are forged out of English Renaissance modes of thought, feeling and attitude, are distanced, apparently deliberately, either in time or space, from specific connections with

Shakespeare's contemporary Elizabethan world. It is partly because of this, that they achieve a free universality of meaning
uncramped by those holding lines which, even in the great
histories, attach the plays to certain particular and fixed Elizabethan
concepts.

King Lear begins as the most "domestic" of the tragedies but it is
also the one which is, though its location is Britain, furthest
removed in time from Shakespeare's own age. The place is
"Britain" not "England", the time is neither contiguously
medieval nor virtually contemporary to Shakespeare. The word
"Britain" itself, if only emotionally, conjures up a remote Celtic
time to which we look for fable prinked only a little by fact,
perhaps pre-Christian in its morality, primitive in its emotions,
stark with the possibility of violence and unnatural deeds. Hazlitt,
writing in 1826, had the right feeling of the play:

> There are no data in history to go upon, no advantage is
> taken of costume, no acquaintance with geography, or
> architecture, or dialect is necessary; but there is an old
> tradition, human nature—an old temple, the human mind—and
> Shakespeare walks into it and looks about him with a lordly
> eye, and seizes on the sacred spoils as his own.[23]

Remote in time and place though it is, *King Lear*, in its exploration of human nature, is blazingly familiar. Its "domesticity"
climbs out of the time where it is placed, and out, therefore, of
myth, and stalks along into the present tense of any reader or
theatregoer who happens upon it. No one who has not lived within
the ebbs and flows of family life can read or see *King Lear* without
being cognisant of its piercing relevance to the geometry of the
ways of blood relationship. In a sense the events it depicts are so
terribly ordinary and familiar. Age, with its slackening of reason,
and its atrophying of sensibility; youth, with its covetousness and
bland self-indulgent assurance—these are the two poles between
which the play voyages, and between which so many families have
foundered. The tragedy of *King Lear* is, of course, the tragedy of
one man, but it is also that of all families who are forced, by circumstance, to make decisions which bring to the surface certain

eternal problems, involving the incompatibility of youth and age:

> Like other aged parents Lear is no gift to good housewifery,
> and there is something poignantly familiar about such a
> one's trudging resentfully to the home of a second daughter.
> 'Age is unnecessary.'[24]

Not least familiar in the play's thematic movement is the demonstration of how little parents know about their own children. This strand in the story of Lear and his daughters brings out an irony which is made all the more intense by the fact that what Lear cannot see is so plain to others and, indeed, to us in the audience. We know Lear's daughters at first better than he knows them just as, perhaps, our neighbour knows our daughter better than we do. The familiar domesticity of the play is very intense and very affecting. The marvel is that the play both expresses the tragedy of the domestic issues *and* transcends them—in the end it is the family of man which has suffered the tragedy.

There is an implied question which precipitates the tragedy. It is put by an old man to his three daughters, and it is probably the most spoken or unspoken query in the history of the family and the families of man. It is the question that lies behind the life and words of Christ and there are few fathers who have not begged, silently or vociferously, for an answer from his progeny. "How much do you love me?"

The play begins with no hint that so much humanity is to be destroyed and given pain by the implications of the separate answers to this question. It is asked not by an enfeebled old man seeking reassurance in the shadow time of his life, but by a king who has the power to command and to give. When we first meet Lear he is not a shuffling relic of greatness but near the height of his power. The court which he commands shines and reverberates with pomp and ceremony.

> Enter one bearing a coronet.

Lear asks,

> Attend the Lords of France and Burgundy.
> [I. I. 33]

True, he talks of conferring his responsibilities on "Younger strength, while we unburthened crawl to death". But his intention is expressed with regal determination and complete clarity of mind and strength of purpose. His intent is "fast", his will is "constant". He has not reached that state of mental decay when anyone could shove him from a purpose which is palpably going to lead to problems. When Kent attempts to do so, his fate is peremptorily settled; each daughter, as she comes forward to present her love, does so with a formal regard not only for parenthood but for the state of kingship. The situation is domestic, certainly, but it is girt about with the trappings of high royalty.

Lear, then, is not senile but he is tainted with weakness. This is compounded of several elements with two dominating. The first is that he transfers into blood relationships the kind of peremptory autocracy he employs, as king, in political relationships. He is really demanding from his daughters the answers he wants; ones that will completely satisfy his expectations. It is the prerogative of kingship, as it is often manifested in Shakespeare's plays, for the monarch not to be crossed in his purposes. Lear makes no allowances for the ties of blood or for the rights of others to interpret what amounts to a rhetorical question in their own way. Lear has, in fact, committed the crime of "unnatural" parenthood before Cordelia speaks words which seem to him to be unnatural. He has put his three children in exactly the same position as a king might put the courtiers surrounding him. Goneril and Regan give the "correct" and expected answers, Cordelia gives the "incorrect", but the truly human and the unexpected reply. The response she gets is one which Lear might have directed to any courtier who had side-stepped an expected reply.

> Mend your speech a little,
> Least you may marre your Fortunes.
> [I. I. 93–4]

It may be recalled that the answer which Cordelia gives is very similar indeed to that of Desdemona to her father. Brabantio asks,

> Do you perceive in all this Noble companie
> Where most you owe obedience?
>
> [I. III. 179–80]

Desdemona replies,

> I do perceive heere a divided dutie.
> To you I am bound for life and education:
> My life and education both do learne me,
> How to respect you. You are the Lord of duty,
> I am hitherto your Daughter. But heere's my Husband:
> And so much dutie, as my Mother shew'd
> To you, preferring you before her Father:
> So much I challenge, that I may professe
> Due to the Moore my Lord.
>
> [I. III. 181–9]

Cordelia's reply to the question,

> Which of you shall we say doth love us most?
> That we, our largest bountie may extend
> Where Nature doth with merit challenge
>
> [I. I 50–2]

is, after the awesome repetition of "nothing",

> Good my Lord,
> You have begot me, bred me, lov'd me.
> I returne those duties backe as are right fit,
> Obey you, Love you, and most Honour you,
> Why have my Sisters Husbands, if they say
> They love you all?
>
> [I. I. 95–8]

Yet, Brabantio's question is far blunter than Lear's. His is the simple request of a simple man, used to being obeyed and expecting obedience. Lear's is the question of a man whose sense of human values is dangerously warped. This is the second and more potentially tragic element in his weakness. His question invites three human beings, tied by blood, to vie with each other for the favour and bounty of a father. He makes the communication of the amount of love they feel for him into a kind of tournament. Even more, his question really invites them to distort their true natures. "Where nature doth with merit challenge" suggests that the award will be in due proportion to the amount of affection they are able to display. If he has made a tournament out of love, he is at the same time making nature into a kind of commodity. He has, in addition to his own unnatural procedure in treating his daughters as if they were servile subjects, the moral weakness which cannot assess true value. He is, in effect, asking for the impossible—he wants, at one and the same time, the most naturally true and the most expectedly satisfactory answer from his daughters. Goneril and Regan find no difficulty in providing the answer. Ironically, in one sense, they are giving Lear the answer that his question deserves, and to this extent, they are responding to the examination truly in the spirit in which it is being conducted. No one whose nature is true and cannot measure either love or merit by Lear's standards could possibly answer the question to his satisfaction. Cordelia's "nothing" is the truest answer to his particular question. For him to accuse her of being "untender", to refer to her as a wretch of "whom nature is ashamed", is the most terrible proof of Lear's basic flaw. He is less guilty of senile stupidity than of a blindness of the spirit. Kent's outburst shows his awareness of Lear's weakness. He says that "power" has "bowed" to "flattery"; he cries out to Lear that the answers he has been given by Goneril and Regan are "empty-hearted". He is well aware of Lear's completely false sense of human values. A phrase of France's, too, shrewdly pinpoints the falseness of the values which Lear is exerting.

> Love's not love
> When it is mingled with regards, that stands
> Aloof from th' intire point.
>
> [I. I. 238–40]

If we doubted false values to be Lear's flaw, his words about Cordelia to Burgundy should quell them. He is still speaking in terms which, by implication, equate "nature" and "commodity".

When she was deare to us, we did hold her so,
But now her price is fallen. Sir, there she stands,
If ought within that little-seeming substance,
Or all of it, with our displeasure piec'd,
And nothing more may fitly like your Grace,
She's there, and she is yours.

[I. I. 196–201]

"Price" and "substance" are the coinage of Lear's estimate of human values.

The first scene of Act One is unique among the tragedies for the comprehensiveness of its information about the nature of the tragic protagonist. We learn all that it is necessary for us to know about the character of Lear to make the ensuing tragic events seem inevitable. Unlike *Macbeth, Othello* and *Hamlet*, where the fatal evidence of weakness is built up slowly and methodically, in this play the facts flare out with a primitive freedom. The inevitability of tragic consequence is assured by what we are taught of the nature of this king. The possible extent of the consequences is suggested to us by a series of other pieces of data. There is Cordelia's banishment, Kent's banishment, but, above all, there are the words of Cordelia about her sisters. What she says is no mere confirmation of the unctuous flattery which they have used upon Lear, but a strong suggestion that this usage is not an isolated example of ill behaviour. Cordelia's speech seems to look back to a time before the play began; it is as if she did not find their flattery in the least surprising.

The Jewels of our Father with wash'd lies
Cordelia leaves you, I know you what you are,
And like a Sister am most loth to call
Your faults as they are named, Love well our Father:
To your professed bosomes I commit him.

[I. I. 268–72]

The parting speeches of Goneril and Regan are superbly modulated by Shakespeare so that any judgements we may have been prepared to make on the sisters, first by their flattery and, second, by

Cordelia's speech, are subject to some doubt. They have not yet
been starkly categorised as evil. Indeed, what they have to say,
given what we have learned of Lear, seems reasonable. In the face
of Lear's caprice we cannot deny that the precautions the two
sisters desire do not seem either illogical or particularly sinister.

> *Gon:* I think our father will hence to night.
> *Reg:* That's most certaine, and with you: next moneth with
> us.
> *Gone:* You see how full of changes his age is, the observation
> we have made of it hath beene little; he alwaies lov'd our
> Sister most, and with what poore judgement he hath now
> cast her off, appeares too grossely.
>
> [I. I. 285–94]

More than this, Goneril and Regan, like Cordelia, seem to look
back to a time before the play begins and give us a context for
Lear's actions. Age may have exaggerated his nature, but it is not
the cause. Shakespeare seems at pains not to attribute Lear's state
of mind and spirit to the accident of age. Shakespeare knew that
the highest tragedy is not a bedfellow of unavoidable accident,
but is the issue of fate and human weakness. The accident of
Lear's age does not explain his actions. This man is blind and
insensitive but he has always been so.

> The best and soundest of his time hath bin' but
> rash, then must we looke from his age, to
> receive not alone the unperfections of long
> ingraffed condition, but there withall the unruly
> way-wardnesse, that infirme and cholericke years
> bring with them.
>
> [I. I. 294–9]

The stage, then, is set for events whose course will be unpredict-
able but whose form is likely to be dark and disquieting. The
whole of scene two of the first Act is concerned with the Edmund/
Gloucester plot which serves, immediately, to give a wider context to the strictly domestic Lear story. It is, of course, a cliché of
criticism that this secondary plot forms a mournful and ironic

obbligato to the main theme. The closeness is established from its first appearance. The deception of parent by child, the animosity between children, the dislocation of the meaning of "nature" (in this case given an additional twist by the fact that Edmund is a bastard), the precipitate haste with which the parent is prepared to think the worst of the child, on the basis of flimsy evidence that is never investigated. Lear and Gloucester even employ a generally similar rhetorical language in speeches which sum up their feelings about the effects of the unnatural deeds their respective children have perpetrated on them. Lear's,

> For the sacred radience of the Sunne,
> The miseries of Heccat and the night:
> By all the operation of the Orbes,
> From whom we do exist, and cease to be,
> Heere I disclaime all my Paternall care,
> Propinquity and property of blood,
> And as a stranger to my heart and me,
> Hold thee from this for ever.
>
> [I. I. 108–15]

is paralleled by Gloucester's,

> These late Eclipses in the Sun and Moone
> portend no good to us: though the wisedome
> of Nature can reason it thus . . .
> Love cooles, friendship falls off, Brothers divide.
> In Cities, mutinies; in Countries, discord;
> in Pallaces, Treason; and the Bond
> Crack'd, 'twixt Sonne and Father.
>
> [I. II. 100–8]

Yet what really binds them together are the limitations of their parental affections; Gloucester's crime is less than Lear's; he could at least declare that the hand of villainy helped to push him into false judgement; yet the threshold of his love for his children is terribly low—his crime, like Lear's, is a failure of the spirit of love. He is truly, as Edmund says, "a credulous father".

One of the most affecting features of the play is the apparent

speed which attends the decay in Lear's status. By Act One, scene
three, the trap he has placed himself in is on the point, already, of
closing on him. Various attempts (as for example in the Variorum
edition)²⁵ to calculate exactly the time taken up by the action,
are inconclusive, largely because the play (unlike *Romeo and Juliet*
for example) is niggardly in its provision of chronological sign-
posts. In any case, a slavish attempt to establish its chronology is
likely to do nothing or little to aid the mounting effect of the play
upon the reader or audience. What is important is the impression,
which begins with the end of Act One, scene two, of a relentless
precipitancy in Lear's fall, and, accompanying it, an access of
increasing isolation for Lear. In Act One, scene three, Goneril can
no longer endure Lear's "riotous" knights, nor the fact that he

> . . . himselfe upbraides us
> On every trifle.
>
> [I. II. 6–7]

We recall Goneril's conversation with her sister at the end of
Act One, scene one, in which they speak of his fickle temperament.
What we have seen of Lear thus far seems only to confirm the
truth of their words. The critical point now reached is that where
we might discover the extent of the sisters' infamy. Are they
merely guilty of expedient flattery or are they prepared to go
much further? When Goneril rails about his knights and Lear's
pernicketiness is she preparing herself for an unwarranted assault
on the foolish fond old king, or is there any justification for her
words? Lear's first words in Act One, scene four, when he returns
(presumably from hunting) to Goneril's home would seem to give
them justification. His words are expressed in the tone and colour
of a bad tempered autocrat.

> Let me not stay a jot for dinner, go get it ready.
>
> [I. IV. 8–9]

The treatment Lear gets from Oswald, in which his dignity and
status are affronted, is no more nor less than a demonstration in
action of Goneril's desire expressed earlier to Oswald:

> Put on what weary negligence you please,
> You and your Fellowes: I'de have it come to question.
>> [I. III. 13–14]

Oswald has been instructed in his behaviour so that the matter should come out into the open. It does so. Goneril speaks reasonably.

> Not only Sir this, your all lycenc'd Foole,
> But other of your insolent retinue
> Do hourely Carpe and Quarrell, breaking forth
> In ranke, and (not to be endur'd) riots Sir.
>
> .   .   .   .
>
> I would you would make use of your good wisedome
> (Whereof I know you are fraught), and put away
> These dispositions, which of late transport you
> From what you rightly are.
>> [I. IV 219–22]

Indeed the keynote of Goneril's passionate attempts to persuade Lear to "disquantity" his knights is exasperation. He is incapable of rational reply to anything she says, and in the end he utters his terrible curse upon her. There are few people who have experienced such a domestic situation who could, if pushed to decide, condemn Goneril completely while absolving Lear. His words, his curse, are a tremendous demonstration of the temperament which at "the best and soundest of his time hath been but rash". The astonishing truth to common experience of the final scene of Act One is even more illustrated by the reaction of Albany to the departure of Lear from his home. However strong the rational grounds for what Goneril has said and suggested, the lingering doubts exist about their rightness.

> I cannot be so partial *Gonerill*,
> To the great love I beare you,
>> [I. IV. 312–13]

> Well, you may feare too farre.
>> [I. IV. 328]

> How farre your eies may pierce I cannot tell;
> Striving to better, oft we marre what's well.
>
> [I. IV. 346–7]

Though not prepared, as yet, to condemn Goneril, the doubts Albany exposes raise an answering chord in our own hearts, and there is something else too. The "love" which Goneril is demonstrating now towards her father is certainly not the love she expressed with such unctuous fluency upon command. If we examine the rationality of her attempts to "disquantity" Lear, what strikes us is, precisely, the reasonableness of it. It is what Hazlitt calls—"cool didactic reasoning".[26] There is no love involved, certainly not the love that was originally declared, and certainly not of that kind which Lear has demanded. Goneril, for her satisfaction and convenience, is demanding of Lear as impossible a self-sacrifice, as utterly servile a response, as he had demanded of her and her two sisters. He asks them, in effect, to disabuse themselves of that element in personality which says—"this is mine to give, and I will give it on my own terms and in my own words". Lear, when he divested himself of the property of kingship wished to maintain the status and appearance of kingship.

> Onely we shall retaine
> The name, and all th' addition to a king.
>
> [I. I. 134–5]

Goneril's requests are a terrible *quid pro quo* for the request made of her by her father, when he gave up his property.

So that by scene four we are less conscious of "guilt" on the part of Goneril, than of the extent to which she is, ironically, her father's daughter. Together, Lear and Goneril and, so far to a lesser extent, Regan, have given us a grim introduction to what lack of true "nature", lack of love that gives more than it takes, means. Thus a terrible irony is created—Lear is beginning to receive no more than he deserves. By the end of scene four the characters have begun to move out of the domestic relationships towards a symbolic state where they stand for aspects of disnature, dislove (to employ a repeated prefix of the play).

The whole of Act Two, scenes one and two, is concerned with externalising, and therefore widening the implications of, the unnatural relationships that have been revealed in the first Act. The use of a forged letter, a pretended wound, and false report (devices very reminiscent of those Shakespeare had recently used in *Othello*) by the doubly-called "unnatural" Edmund, serve to put this melancholy condition into the category of a crime. Edmund's actions are, in a way, a proof that disnature is not a merely static quality, but is capable of active and sinister movement. The putting to flight of his brother widens and activates what, in the Lear story so far, has been like the grumbling of a half sleeping volcano. The later blinding of Gloucester, in which Regan plays a positive and leading part, serves not only to deepen the sinister and cruel context of disnature, but to point, most horribly, through her, the parallel situations of Gloucester and of Lear.

The first four scenes of the second Act clearly distinguish, too, between the characters of Goneril and Regan, and between their domestic environments. Goneril, at first, is cruel by default rather than apparent will. Her default is a lack of true love and a lack of intelligence. Her letter to Regan is her chief actual crime. It prepares the more subtle and dangerous woman for positive action. Regan, ironically, has all her father's peremptory autocracy.

> I have this present evening from my Sister
> Beene well inform'd of them, and with such Cautions,
> That if they were to sojourne at my house,
> Ile not be there.
>
> [II. I. 101–4]

The court in which she is a dominant figure seems, by comparison with Goneril's, rife with potential cruelty, faction and intrigue. In marrying Albany a weak woman has met a weak man. In marrying Cornwall a dangerous and very intelligent sadist has joined with one who has a great stomach for cruelty. For Shakespeare seems to go out of his way to make Regan into a sadist. It is she who increases, with a curious relish, Kent's sentence in the stocks.

> Till noone? till night my Lord, and all night too.
>   [II. II. 130]

And although textual difficulties make it uncertain whether they
are her words, what we know of her strongly suggests that it is she
who says of Kent in the stocks,

> Put in his legs.
>   [II. II. 145]

If we had any doubts about her sadism, the blinding of Gloucester
would remove them. She instructs the ropes to be bound "hard,
hard". It is more than likely that it is she who commits the indig-
nity on Gloucester of pulling his beard. She cries out for Gloucester's
other eye to be put out; she kills the remonstrating servant from
behind; she, it is, who says of Gloucester,

> Go thrust him out at gates, and let him smell
> His way to Dover.
>   [III. VII. 92–3]

The justification for thus dwelling on the sadism of this creature,
is that its presence differentiates her so strongly from her sister.
The difference between them is often ignored and they are played
as if the evil they each harbour is of an entirely similar colouring.
Regan's evil is, at first, far more active than Goneril's. The
atmosphere she engenders around her is, initially, more dangerous; it is through Regan rather than Goneril that we learn that
"disnature" is not only inhuman but capable of being evil. Yet,
finally, Goneril out-paces Regan, climbing slowly but inexorably
into criminality, while the other, having swiftly revealed her
vicious side, falls a victim to some unknown disease (conscience?)
then to a poison administered by Goneril.

For the first two scenes of Act Two Lear is absent from the
action. It is noticeable that in all four of the great tragedies Shakespeare removes the protagonist for some considerable time. No
doubt practical considerations were involved; any actor playing
these parts needs breathing space from the mere physical and
intellectual demands of the role. Yet Shakespeare hardly ever

misses the opportunity to make capital out of such necessity. In the case of *Hamlet, Othello* and *Macbeth* and, it may be added, most conspicuously in *Richard II*, the opportunity is taken either to give additional information from others about the protagonist or to condition us for some change in the protagonist which is manifest when he next appears. In the case of Hamlet, Othello and Macbeth there is a change, in the case of Lear himself there is not. When he reappears in Act Two, scene four, he is still the ranting self-pitying man we have seen previously.

> The King would speak with Cornwall,
> The deere Father
> Would with his Daughter speake, commands,
>   tends, service,
> Are they inform'd of this?
>
> [II. IV. 99–101]

It is not until the end of the scene immediately before his exit into the storm that he speaks words whose effect is to begin to change our feelings about and towards him. Lear, albeit faintly, shows signs of reaching inside himself for something other than what he has revealed before. His wayward, narrow spirit, discovers a nobility and a certain courage. For the first time his self-indulgence begins to transform into a quality which begets our sympathy. He does not ask the gods to take vengeance on his behalf, but to teach him "patience" and "noble anger". It is true that the wilder part of him still bursts forth as when he cries,

> No you unnatural Hags,
> I will have such revenges on you both.
>
> [II. IV. 277–8]

but even in his wildness, the seeds of that kind of noble fortitude which he is going to need and reveal later on begin to generate.

> You thinke Ile weepe,
> No, Ile not weepe, I have full cause of weeping,
> But this heart shal break into a hundred thousand flawes
> Or ere Ile weepe.
>
> [II. IV. 281–5]

Immediately before his advance into the storm where his reason will be beleagered and eventually capitulate, Lear is suddenly presented to us in a new light. We become prepared for pity as surely as he is being prepared to go through the darkness.

Preparations for our change of attitude have in fact begun before, not directly, but by subtle indications. It is achieved through three agencies. First by the concentration on the story of Gloucester during Lear's absence which almost ousts, for a time, the Lear story from the action. Our imaginations are conditioned, before we meet Lear again, to react towards the treachery of Edmund and the mental blindness of Gloucester. We are already conditioned, that is, to the idea of filial treachery. This, as yet unconsciously, is preparing our sensibilities in the direction of sympathy for all victims of such treachery. When these victims (however much we find blame in them) are seen to be gradually isolated, the possibility of sympathy is further increased. Paradoxically, in Lear's case, this isolation is furthered by the very two people who, physically and intellectually, never forsake him— Kent and the Fool. These are the two other agencies by which our attitude to Lear is caused to change. Kent knew the dangers of Lear's actions as they were being performed in the first scene of Act One. His blunt, honest sense of duty, and his caring humanity shine like gold in the multiplying dross of the society that surrounds Lear. In Kent, Lear, in simple terms, has a doughty champion and friend whose resolution to succour the king will never fail. Yet, curiously, Kent's very directness of word and deed serves to increase the fractious relationships between Lear and his daughters. In his determination to speak truth, Kent exacerbates the situation. His handling of Oswald, justified though it may be by Oswald's studied insolence, is incautious. His words to Cornwall before he is put in the stocks are hardly calculated (considering he is known as Lear's servant) to decrease Cornwall and Regan's determination to rid Lear of his unruly attendants. When Lear appears and discovers Kent in the stocks, the nature of his replies to the king raises the temperature of Lear's mind and heart.

Lear: What's he,
   That hath so much thy place mistooke
   To set thee heere?
Kent: It is both he and she,
   Your Son, and Daughter.
Lear: No.
Kent: Yes.
Lear: No I say.
Kent: I say yea.
Lear: By Juppiter I sweare no.
Kent: By Juno, I sweare I.
                    [II. IV. 11–21]

The Fool, no less than Kent, but with a pungency of illustration, wit and truth, increases Lear's temper.

Fool: If I gave them all my living, I'ld keepe my Coxcombes
   my selfe, there's mine, beg another of thy Daughter.
Lear: Take heed Sirrah, the whip.
Fool: Truth's a dog must to kennell, hee
   must be whipt out, when the Lady
   Brach may stand by' th' fire and stinke.
                    [I. IV. 106–12]

The Fool we meet in his first encounter with Lear is no mere purveyor of innuendoes, half-hidden hints. He goes directly to the mark. He is fulfilling absolutely the aspirations of Jaques in *As You Like It*. He is attempting to "cleanse the foul body" of Lear's infected mind. He is also fulfilling exactly the function of the true Fool in that his shafts are given irony by wry humour. What is so conspicuously lacking in Lear and in all his progeny is a sense of humour, of wit. As Wilson Knight says,

If Lear could laugh—if the Lears of the world could laugh at themselves—there would be no such tragedy.[27]

The Fool attempts to purge with truth, whose message is—see how absurd the situation is in which you have placed yourself; but Lear is unable to hear the message because a self-indulgent sense of

status and dignity has atrophied his sense of the difference between
what is absurdly wrong and what is absolutely right, proper and
human.

The Fool, then, in the first two Acts, joins the Edmund/
Gloucester plot and Kent as agents which, at one and the same
time, ironically exacerbate the conditions for tragedy *and* increase
the possibilities of our eventually achieving the right grounds for
pity.

There is a distinct and, in its implications, immense break in the
atmosphere and the form of this play at the beginning of Act
Three. Up to this point the "domestic" nature of the events has
predominated; dark tragedy which will engulf both the inner and
outer lives of men has barely been hinted at. Indeed, like *Romeo and
Juliet* and like *Othello* there is something curiously "absurd" about
the events. They are cavilling; they are the result of somewhat
petty inflexibilities of mind and self-indulgence. The crises created
could, we believe, easily be reversed by the exercise of simple
reason. The events and crises are familiar; they do not involve the
interventions of the supernatural. One has observed and heard of
such domestic stupidities in everyday life and one has marvelled
that people should be so crass as to refuse to see the relatively simple
way to redress their absurdity.

The very first words of Act Three take us into darker, stranger
countries of experience. The language used by Kent and the
Gentleman on the heath has a startling effect.

> *Kent:* Who's there besides foule weather?
> *Gon:* One minded like the weather, most unquietly.
> [III. I. 1–2]

For the first time the elements and man's mind are equated. Certainly, we have had in the previous two Acts Lear's raging in
which the heavens, the gods and nature have been invoked. Yet all
this was the grand rhetoric of mood. Now, Lear is not invoking.
Even before we see him he seems to have become a victim and a
confidant of nature itself. In another part of the heath where the
storm shakes the earth, we meet Lear. His great speech in which he
addresses the elements is no mere invocation. It is as if he is in the

process of total identification with natural catastrophe. The problem for the actor in this great speech has been taken to be one of
producing enough volume to do justice to the extraordinary
"impersonation" of a storm which the words and images are
creating. The onomatopoeia of lines like

> Blow windes, and crack your cheeks; Rage, blow
> You Cataracts, and Hyrricanos spout,
> Till you have drench'd our Steeples, drown the Cockes.
> You Sulph'rous and Thought-executing Fires,
> Vaunt-curriors of Oake-cleaving Thunder-bolts,
> Sindge my white head
>
> [III. II. 1–6]

are immensely difficult to match in voice. The tremendous piling
up of phrase after phrase, like the terrible growing architecture of a
storm, adds to the actor's task.

With modern electronic and mechanical aids, the actor can be
helped, but, in the final analysis, the onus is upon him. Indeed too
much mechanical aid can be as much of a liability as none at all.
The reason is that it is not simply that the actor, in purely technical
terms, is asked to "impersonate" a storm, but that, in a sense, Lear
and the storm have become identified. This speech is the proof
positive of the immense change in form and atmosphere that the
play has taken. Lear is no longer a foolish old man; the dramatist
has plucked him out of domestic familiarity and made of him a
great symbol. From Act Three to the end we no longer think of
Lear in terms of his original guilt, or his mental blindness; neither
do we ever regard him simply as a realised character in a play. He
seems to have been made to transcend both himself and the confines of what we call dramatic form. The effect of the storm scene
is to make us forget the particularities of the play's dramatic action
and to be engulfed by an experience of human suffering utterly
naked in its presentation. Yet the very phrase "human suffering"
is a poor cypher to stand for the complexity of what happens in
the heath scene. Lear's self-identification with the storm almost
totally purges him of his passion. It begins to drop away leaving
him with a grieving quietude against whose sadness the jingling

words of the Fool play ironically. The Fool reminds him and us of
the particularities of his case while Lear is slowly entering into a
condition where his whole inner being is to be changed. It is like a
tin whistle playing at a great man's obsequies.

> *Lear:* Come on my boy. How dost my boy? Art cold?
>   I am cold my selfe . . .
>   The Art of our Necessities is strange,
>   And can make rude things precious . . .
>
> .   .   .   .
>
> *Fool:* He that has and a little-tyne wit,
>   With heigh-ho, the Winde and the Raine,
>   Must make content with his Fortunes fit,
>   Though the Raine it raineth every day.
>   [III. II. 68–78]

Kent's arrival, and his mention of the storm, bring Lear again to
passion, but it is a poor thing now compared to its former appearance. The purging is terrible; its final spasm is agonising to contemplate and, for the first time, we can completely accept even
Lear's self-pity.

> I am a man
> More sinn'd against, then sinning.
>   [III. II. 59]

We accept it now, when before we did not, because the play has
moved from a depiction of mere plot into an embodiment of
human suffering.

The Fool continues to jingle his ironic *obbligato* to events that
are now happening inside Lear's very soul. Passion which was
formerly the very pith of Lear's personality is vanquished in him.
He can find nothing yet to take its place, and so

> My wits begin to turne.
>   [III. II. 67]

Yet they do not yet completely fall away from him. When Kent
reappears and asks Lear to enter the hovel, we have the first positive indication of the changes that are happening inside him. He

shouts out "filial ingratitude", he threatens that he will "punish home". But these cries are a mere vagrant flotsam and jetsam of the old wild Lear. As soon as he has cried them he says,

> O that way madness lies; let me shun that;
> No more of that.
>
> [III. IV. 21–2]

He has rejected passion. Kent repeats his request that he should enter the hovel. The answer he gets—utterly simple in its expression—is profound in its implications.

> Prythee, go in thy selfe, seeke thine owne ease.
>
> [III. IV. 23]

The peremptory man, accustomed to first place and to obedience, puts another one before him. This line is a direct and moving proof, expressed in simple personal terms, of what it is that is beginning to replace passion in King Lear. Lear, alone, while the others clamber into the hovel, tells us and himself what it is.

> Take Physicke, Pompe,
> Expose thy self to feele what wretches feele,
> That thou maist shake the superflux to them,
> And shew the Heavens more just.
>
> [III. IV. 33–5]

Yet the shock to his system which is compounded of what Goneril and Regan have done, and the spiritual metamorphosis that is occurring in him, is too much for him to bear. His wits, indeed, now do begin to turn. The manner of their turning and the advent of Edgar as Poor Tom signal an even further departure of this play from conventional dramatic modes. At the height of the storm Lear identied himself with it and, as it died away, so did his passion. Now, he comes to identify himself with the "madness" of Tom, and as it increases its whirligig presence, so Lear's wits increase their distance from reason—he has now begun to identify himself with madness. The Fool and Kent stand helplessly by while Lear, with a kind of muted, almost half-contented frenzy, begins to walk with madness. The theatrical impact of this is uniquely strange and compelling. There is nothing in European drama which gives us anything approaching this experience. The movement of the scene has a mesmeric effect. We seem not to be in the presence of stage characters, but in the midst of an enveloping pattern of rhythm and sound. Edgar's speeches sway in a kind of demented liturgy; Lear's responses are, for the most part, staccato and intellectually numbed; the Fool's little pipe of reason whistles with ever-growing ineffectiveness. Kent speaks only one sentence—this blunt man from the world of humans is almost an irrelevancy in this supranatural place and time. Gloucester's arrival comes between us and the spell that has been woven about us, but we can still hear it. At the very end of scene four, Edgar and Lear have joined in a pitiful consanguinity. A kind of agonised wit comes into Lear's distempered mind; he has all the confiding, urgent, almost chuckling content which we see in the deranged, who begin to create their own worlds with their own rules, and to people them with their own creations.

> *Lear:*   O cry you mercy, Sir:
>   Noble Philosopher, your company.
> *Edg:* Tom's a cold.
>
>   .   .   .   .
>
> *Lear:* Come, let's in all.
> *Kent:* This way, my Lord.
> *Lear:*   With him;
>   I will keepe still with my Philosopher.
>
>   [III. IV. 167–72]

In scene six, this process of creation has proceeded one stage further. Lear puts himself at the head of his new world, and proceeds to arraign its recalcitrant citizens.

If we marvel at Shakespeare's achievement in scene four where Lear seems, as has been said, to step out of the territories of mere drama, what word can be used to describe the skill by which, in scene six, he maintains the strange, unique atmosphere and, at the same time, begins to remind us that what we have seen and experienced does have its source somewhere in familiar event and motivation. We have been pulled away from the particularities of Goneril, Regan and Edmund and have seen the human spirit naked in agony; now the particularities begin to swirl and their coming serves to give the agony a terrible and moving point of reference. In scene six Lear, in his arraignment of the citizens of his new dark world, drifts in and out of reason and reality. It is as if we see his mind opening and closing, with intermittent light attempting desperately to vanquish the darkness. Sometimes he is a child.

> *Fool:* Prythee, Nunkle, tell me, whether a madman be a
>   Gentleman, or a Yeoman?
> *Lear:* A king, a king.
>
> > [III. IV. 9–11]

Sometimes he has the quick but wild authority of the deranged.

> It shalbe done; I wil arraigne them straight,
>   come, sit thou here, thou most learned Justice.
>
> > [III. VI. 20]

Sometimes, in his dark mind, Goneril appears, but it is another Lear she has wronged.

> Arraigne her first to Goneril, I here take
>   my oath before this honorable assembly kickt
>   the poore king her father.
>
> > [III. VI. 46–8]

And once, his mind wanders into the past and it is he himself who is the victim.

> Then let them Anatomise Regan:
>   See what breeds about her heart. Is
>   there any cause in Nature that make
>   these hard-hearts.
>
> > [III. VI. 75–7]

There is created a terrible contrapuntal effect between delusion and reality. It is an indictment not only of the idea of human cruelty, but of the particular facts of the cruelty that has been practised on Lear. The dramatic balance is perfect—the play, in these two scenes, has trodden superbly and unerringly between poetic symbolism and theatrical reality.

In Act Three, scene seven, the play turns, for a time, to the domestic familiarities of the first two Acts. The scathing revenge on Gloucester, the news of the landing of the King of France's army, the implications of a sexual relationship between Edmund and Goneril, the wounding of Cornwall—all these matters are concentrated into a short sharp time, and the effect is, first, to re-establish fully the realistic cause and effect plot line and, second, to imply, as Shakespeare so inevitably does in his tragedies, how evil and cruelty are never contained, but always spread.

The blinding of Gloucester, on stage, has been condemned as unnecessary. It is indeed, not often that Shakespeare, in his plays, so explicitly and starkly depicts such bestial cruelty. Yet, to accuse him of specious sensationalism is to ignore a particular effect of the scene. Just as in the Cinna the Poet scene in *Julius Caesar*, Shakespeare uses direct cruelty for a purpose beyond itself. The servant who, when Gloucester cries for help, says,

> Hold your hand, my Lord
> I have serv'd you ever since I was a Childe:
> But better service have I never done you,
> Then now to bid you hold
>
> [III. VII. 72–4]

is the embodiment of the scene's purpose. It is the reality of human pity as much as the fact of human cruelty that the scene is intended to display; just as in *Julius Caesar* when Cinna cries,

> I am Cinna the Poet
> [III. III. 30]

it is the irony of human misjudgement as much as the fact of mob violence that is calculated to effect this. After the blinding of Gloucester, the emotions and practices of revenge and cruelty which inhabit Goneril and Regan's world begin to turn inward. Over a series of scenes we witness the piece by piece disintegration of their world through outward pressures, through sexual jealousies, through hatred and distrust. Indeed, after the

Gloucester scene, the play presents clear divisions of interest, effect and mode. The Goneril/Regan scenes present domestic broil; the scenes in which Cordelia and her husband are presented have a spirit of amity, of succour and love; the scenes between Edgar and his father are used in order to introduce, very directly, the element of healing, of kindness, filial love and the expunging of Gloucester's mental blindness. Lear, alone, until he is rescued and recognises Cordelia, belongs to none of these categories. Shakespeare very deliberately keeps him isolated—he wanders, fitfully, through the air, having consort with people, but in essence, utterly by himself. It is as if while the action itself is moving towards a state where evil may be overcome, and where the forces of cruelty which have been shown are being replaced by their opposite, Lear is disconnected. The world is moving in a certain direction, but it seems to move past him—it is as if he is a creature moving without purpose in a stream whose different currents and eddies have no effect on him. He is himself, alone.

His mind still flickers with light, but very fitfully. Yet there are certain things about this mad Lear which are above and beyond mere madness. In his meandering words we discover that the purging which destroyed most of his sanity has given him, paradoxically, a clarity of truth, not only about the events which led to his state, but about the whole world and its ways. If he had said in Act One, scene one, what he says in Act Four, scene six:

> Ha! Gonerile with a white beard? They flatter'd me like a
> Dogge, and told mee I had the white hayres in my Beard,
> ere the black ones were there. To say I, and no, to everything
> that I said: I, and no too, was no good Divinity.
>
> [IV. VI. 96–9]

he would not have suffered, and there would have been no tragedy. If he had had the "wit" in Act One, scene one, to see his kingship in the way he sees it in Act Four, scene six, he would not have been fond, foolish, autocratic and narrow-minded. If he had had the sensitivity of mind and feeling to know the difference between natural love and commodity-love in Act One, scene one, he would have known which of his daughters spoke the truth. In Act

Four, scene six, he knows the difference clearly, for he has been taught to observe the ways of the world.

> What, art mad? a man may see how this world goes, with no eyes. Looke with thine eares: see how your Justice railes upon yond simple theefe. Hearke in thine eare: Change places, and handy—dandy, which is the Justice, which is the theefe.
>
> [IV. VI. 150–4]

Lear has, indeed, learned wisdom. Yet no amount of sifting through his mad later scenes to discover the abstract "developments" which have occurred in the character, can equal in importance the effect of experiencing him as a theatrical presence. It is almost unbearable to support the variety of emotions which his presence arouses in us. He is so many things. He becomes the communicator of that wry, clipped poetry in which Shakespeare seems to be able to harness images and concepts, in themselves incompatible, but miraculously joined to speak harsh truths.

> No, the Wren goes too't, and the small gilded Fly
> Do's letcher in my sight. Let Copulation thrive.
> For Gloucesters bastard son was kinder to his Father,
> Then my Daughters got 'tweene the lawfull sheets.
> Too't Luxury pell-mell . . .
>
> [IV. VI. 112–16]

He is, at times, like some embittered sage, mocking the world with ironic truth.

> *Glou:* O let me kisse that hand.
> *Lear:* Let me wipe it first,
>   It smells of Mortality.
>
> [IV. VI. 132–3]

He is, fleetingly, like a child again, but one grown old in cynicism.

> *Gent:* You shall have any thing.
> *Lear:* No Seconds? All my selfe?
>
> [IV. VI. 195]

Towards the end, he wrings our hearts by his gentle vulnerability, his fearful gratitude, his frail dignity.

> Pray do not mocke me:
> I am a very foolish fond old man,
> Fourscore and upward,
> Not an hour more, nor lesse:
> And to deale plainely,
> I feare I am not in my perfect mind.
> [IV. VII. 59–63]

It is because the character of Lear is made to arouse in us such a maelstrom of emotion that it is difficult to come to a conclusion about what we call the "philosophical" implications. One's mind veers from concluding that the experience we have had is in itself too various and huge to allow of intellectual formalisation, to a conviction, so powerful is the play, that Shakespeare intends us to come away having found a particular intellectual decision. Critics, over the centuries, have ranged themselves fairly equally on opposite sides. For some, the play, piling on evidences of cruelty upon cruelty, subjecting, as it does, one man to the uttermost purging of his soul and then depriving him of the benefits of the purge, is a vision of a desperately meaningless universe. To others, the filial love of Edgar, the radiant truth of Cordelia, the very purging of Lear so that he achieves wisdom, dignity and an awareness of true love, cancels out the spectacle of mankind's darker side. For some the play is the nearest Shakespeare ever came to presenting an "absurd" view of the universe; for others it is an affirmation of Christian faith—man pays a price for guilt, inhumanity, and the penance is hard, but the outcome is a reconciliation and peace.[28]

Yet, so often what we experience in the theatre, is at variance with what intellectual probing discovers. The end of the play cannot, as we watch it, either be said to be to be happy or sad, dismissive or affirmative. We experience a rare and touching joy when Cordelia is re-united with her father; we suffer a corresponding grief when that re-uniting is smashed by a death which, if Edmund had spoken moments earlier, might have been avoided. We share the quiet frail satisfaction of Lear in recognising his daughter, yet we are forced almost to avert our eyes and stop our ears.

The self-sacrifice of Kent who determines to follow his master into the grave seems, to us, both a joyful affirmation of love and duty and, at the same time, a grievous happening. Edgar's assumption of authority is a logically right representation of the restoration of order and humanity, yet, like the coming of Fortinbras, fails to wipe out from our minds and imaginations what we have experienced. Indeed Edgar's final words sum up the truth of our experience.

> The waight of this sad time we must obey,
> Speake what we feele, not what we ought to say:
> The oldest hath borne most, we that are yong,
> Shall never see so much, nor live so long.
>
> [v. III. 322–6]

Much of the play's reality is encased within these lines. Of all Shakespeare's tragedies this is the one we apprehend most through our feelings; what our intelligence tells us that we ought to reflect upon—its "philosophical" meanings—is overborn by the emotions. The very pith of our emotional experience is created from the spectacle of old age suffering so much and so long. However old we may be we leave the play convinced that no man has ever lived so long or suffered so much as King Lear. His tragedy is, in its essence, therefore, that of Mankind itself, the extent of whose tenancy of this planet is incommensurate with the amount of love, wisdom and humanity it has acquired. It is neither optimistic nor pessimistic, but an immense evocation of the reality of human existence. We would not be human if we were not cruel, faithless and treacherous, but we would be more human if we more closely harboured love, reason and fidelity.

Macbeth

Macbeth is Shakespeare's most haunting play. It not only stirs but frightens the imagination. In a sense it is also the "favourite" play of many readers and theatregoers. There is a connection between what it does to the imagination and its attraction for it. There are certain places, certain books, certain pieces of music, certain pictures, certain people, which, when we meet or recall them, energise our emotions in a particular way. They cause them to rise to a point almost beyond tolerance. While we are caught within their power almost anything seems possible; they have no limits to them and we cannot say—"Here are the boundaries of what we seem capable of experiencing from these things."

Macbeth, perhaps especially when we read it, gives us many moments when the play seems capable of leaping from the page, embodying itself into some monstrous shape which will engulf us. Perhaps, indeed, the power of the play rests in its curious ability to make us believe, even in reading, that it will come alive. When we read of Macbeth's slow walk, with bloodstained hands, from Duncan's chamber, he escapes from the edges of the page, and we are inclined to look about us to see if he is standing there.

Any inclination to dismiss this effect as idle fancy can be given pause by reflecting upon the play's strange status in the history of theatre. Not only does it escape from the printed page and haunt our waking senses, but it has, in a sense, escaped from the confines of the workaday theatre itself. All actors treat *Macbeth* with awesome respect, not only because it is a great play but because so many performances throughout history have been accompanied by tragic, sinister, and disquieting events. Coincidence is a mere word which we conveniently use to shove off what is often inexplicable. The stage history of *Macbeth*[29] is full of "coincidences" in which death, accident, and strange occurrences figure large.

The play is about evil and, however we attempt to explain or dismiss its aura in theatre history, it seems to generate an evil atmosphere both in the reader and in the actor. Clairvoyance may provide its own explanations; criticism is obliged to inquire whether this play is, in any one or in a number of ways, unique in Shakespeare's canon.

There is one certain quality which distinguishes it from all the other plays. This is the language. It is memorable language in the sense that it sticks in the mind in a manner quite distinct from the rest. The imagery is more consistently "pictorial" than in any

D

other play; it is, moreover, more redolent and evocative of action than any other play. There are few lines in which any character speaks, as it were, reflectively, without his thoughts implying tremendous action, either of the mind or of the body. Thought, and what it leads to in human movement, have become one in this play. When we hear Hamlet speculate upon life and death, we join with him in speculation; he gives us an intellectual and emotional exposition of a point of view:

> To be, or not to be, that is the Question:
> Whether 'tis Nobler in the minde to suffer
> The Slings and Arrowes of outragious Fortune,
> Or to take Armes against a Sea of troubles,
> And by opposing end them.
>
> [III. I. 56–60]

When Macbeth weighs up the pros and cons of killing Duncan, the deed itself and the immense voyaging of his hot imagination catches us, and we are forced to follow him not speculatively, but with every nerve and sinew full of the expectation of what may happen.

> If it were done, when 'tis done, then 'twer well,
> If were done quickly: if th' Assassination
> Could trammell up the Consequence, and catch
> With his surcease, Successe: that but this blow
> Might be the be all, and the end all. Heere,
> But heere, upon this Bank and Schoole of time,
> Wee'ld jump the life to come.
>
> [I. VII. I–7]

The language of the play does indeed "Blow the horrid deed in every eye"—we see it, and we feel it. Every soliloquy Macbeth speaks is not only, of itself, pictorial and active, but threatens action, and what it threatens is always evil. George Hunter's phrase that "The play is a discovery or anatomy of evil", does not, for all its truth, require the alternative—it is all "discovery".

Again, in no other play of Shakespeare is the supernatural so malevolent and so starkly presented. The presence of three witches seems so apt as a dank background to the evil that is generated by Macbeth's own thoughts and deeds, that we tend to suspend our twentieth-century scepticism. We tolerate the benevolent super-naturals of *A Midsummer Night's Dream*, the symbolic appearances in *The Tempest*, because their presence leads to satisfactory and pleasing conclusions—our innate scepticism is allayed by joy. In *Hamlet, Richard III* and *Julius Caesar*, however, the supernatural elements, in the final analysis, seem no more than additives which we ourselves could, without qualm, dismiss from our experience of the play; even the Ghost of Hamlet's father cannot quite escape our tendency to be sceptical, irritated, or even faintly amused. Not so the witches. The fact that they are "weird sisters", and not described as "ghosts", in itself gives them a status disquietingly near to "the natural". Like Hamlet's father their appearance is described in detail, but unlike him, they seem to have an inter-course with human affairs which is constant, close, and male-volent. They do not come intermittently out of hell's regions to descant upon what has happened to them in life, and to grieve loudly about the sufferings of the unaneled; they live within man's society, seizing the thumbs of a shipwrecked sailor, killing swine, taking revenge upon a sailor's wife with chestnuts in her lap, and meeting with victorious soldiers upon a blasted heath in Scotland.

Their presence makes the supernatural curiously domestic. They are around the next bend in the dark lane and not amor-phously appearing out of graves at midnight. Their power is ambivalently expressed in the play. George Hunter claims that "The mode of evil they can create is potential only, not actual, till the human agent takes it inside his mind and makes it his own by a motion of the will".[30] This is true, but only to an extent. Their ability to influence the fate of the master of the Tiger, would seem to have little to do with *his* "will". It is the First Witch who will "Drain him dry as hay", who will withhold sleep from him, who will cause him to "dwindle, peak and pine". It may be argued, as indeed Hunter does, that only when Macbeth wills it, will the evil which they exemplify and demonstrate, become active. Yet we have to remember that they are "active" in that they appear before him on the first occasion. He does not call them up, any more than

Banquo does. It is surely the case that they activate, by the fore-knowledge they have, the seeds of evil ambition which exist, as yet unfertilised, in Macbeth's mind. It is clear that these seeds *are* present. After Ross and Angus confirm the witches' prophecies about his elevation to the Thanedom of Cawdor, Macbeth, in his asides, brings to the surface his secret expectations.

> Glamys, and Thane of Cawdor:
> The greatest is behinde.
>   [I. III. 116–17]

> Two Truths are told
> As happy Prologues to the swelling Act
> Of the Imperiall Theame.
>   [I. III. 127–8]

One of the most teasing critical questions in the play concerns how much Macbeth is "influenced" towards evil by his own will, how much by the witches, and how much by his wife. Criticism has adumbrated theorem after theorem, allotting different factors to each. What is rarely taken into account is the nature of Macbeth's immediate reaction to the prophecies—that is, before he has met his wife after receiving honours. He is in a state of turmoil. Apart from the asides which reveal the secret ambitions, he displays a bewildered reaction. He wants the witches to tell him more, he wishes they had stayed; he turns to Banquo as if for confirmation and asks "And Thane of Cawdor too, went it not so?" He is like a child whose secret dreams seem to be on the point of becoming realities, and is unable to believe it. In his disturbed state he rationalises. The prophecies cannot be either ill or good. He balances "ill" against "good" and they cancel each other out.

> This supernaturall sollisiting
> Cannot be ill; cannot be good.
> If ill? why hath it given me earnest of successe
>
> .   .   .   .
>
> If good? why doe I yeild to that suggestion,
> Whose horrid Image doth unfixe my Heire,
>   [I. III. 130–5]

The state he eventually arrives at before he meets Duncan and, importantly, before he meets his wife, is one of almost totally inactive acceptance. He has pushed to the surface his secret thoughts, he has had one of them confirmed, he has concluded that the prophecies have no moral value, being neither ill nor good— they merely "are". It is chance that has come to roost; time and the hour will run through the roughest day. Only one caveat to inactive waiting remains. He wants to talk over what has happened, at some time, with Banquo when

> The Interim having weigh'd it, let us speake
> Our free Hearts each to other.
>
> [I. III. 154-5]

The Macbeth we meet before he rejoins his wife is, basically, a morally weak man. His military prowess is certain, his status in the hierarchy of Scotland is lofty, his reputation assured. Yet we have strong hints that he has little will-power over his baser instincts. What we witness is a present-tense revelation of the vulnerable interior of a man of high place; a sort of revelation which latterly we only come to know in the posthumous biographies of our leaders. The tone of his letter to his wife echoes his weakness. It is tentative, giving the impression that he requires some strong catalyst to make him come to a decision one way or the other for "ill" or "good". He writes that he "stood rapt in the wonder of it" when he heard the witches' prophecies. He adds, "This have I thought good to deliver thee, my dearest partner of greatness"— as if to say "now, you can make the decision for me". His weakness is underlined by the first words Lady Macbeth speaks after reading the letter. She fears his "nature", she attributes the softer virtues to him of wanting status without being prepared to accept that it cannot be gained without "illness". Soon, he appears and his first words only serve to emphasise his tentative condition.

> My dearest Love,
> Duncan comes here to Night.
>
> [I. IV. 55]

Behind this statement lies one of the most potent hidden questions in the whole of Shakespeare's plays. He is really asking "What shall we do?" It is significant that when she comes out with a plain statement of intention—"He that is coming must be provided for" —he falls back into the same mood that possessed him after he had decided to leave all to chance, yet told Banquo that they should speak about the prophecies on another occasion. He says to his wife, "We will speak further", which echoes his earlier words:

> The *Interim* having weigh'd it, let us speake
> Our free Hearts each to other.
>
> [I. III. 154-5]

At his first meeting with his wife, Macbeth is at his most indecisive. The better part of him is not strong enough to dismiss its opposite. Still no decision has been made in his perplexed mind, and Lady Macbeth has not yet summoned up all her power to push his "compunctious visitings" away. In fact, after Duncan has arrived, he achieves the nearest point to grasping "good" rather than "ill". The soliloquy beginning "If it were done when 'tis done" reveals to us, for the first time, that if Macbeth is weak in will, he is strong both in intelligence and, particularly, imagination. The soliloquy is, as it were, a proof of his ability to know what "good" is, just as his soliloquy before the murder of Duncan is a proof of his imaginative ability to know the reality of evil. His arguments for not doing the deed are comprehensive and subtle. First, they are self-indulgent; he would do the deed *if* the *act* of doing had no consequences, if it were insulated from both past and future, so that no judgement on it were possible. Second, they are conventionally honourable—you do not kill either as a "subject" or "kinsman". Third, again according to convention, as host your duty is to protect not destroy your guest. Fourth, Duncan is a good man. Fifth, such a deed would be an offence to heaven. Finally, he becomes subjective again, and "knows" that the sole justification for such a deed is "vaulting ambition" which will end only in a fall for himself.

The witches have done no more than objectivise secret ambitions; they have not prompted him to act. His wife, as yet, has not played her ace card. That card alone is responsible for forcing him to declare his own hand, and it is one which is starkly simple in its potency. It changes the whole direction of Macbeth's relationship, both to himself and to the whole society in which he lives. After he has concluded that the only reason for killing Duncan is "vaulting ambition" she reappears. She attacks his love and his manhood.

> what Beast was't then
> That made you breake this enterprize to me?
> When you durst do it, then you were a man:
> And to be more then what you were, you would
> Bee so much more the man.
> [I. VII. 47–51]

This has softened him up for the final attack. It is at this point that Macbeth is irrevocably changed from the wavering, tentative being we have seen so far into, first a potential, then an actual, strong murderous man. The change is achieved by Lady Macbeth through the simple expedient of showing how easy the deed will be. In the plethora of critical exposition of Macbeth's state of mind up to the murder of Duncan, it is often forgotten that this man is a soldier—a very successful one—and that, given a logistic situation, he is eminently capable of solving it. He knows the art and craft of professional killing in massed battle. To kill one man in itself is a simplicity for him. Lady Macbeth plays her card—it is an order of battle.

> ... when Duncan is asleepe,
> (Whereto the rather shall his dayes hard Journey
> Soundly invite him) his two Chamberlaines
> Will I with Wine and Wassell, so convince,
> That Memorie, the Warder of the Braine,
> Shall be a Fume, and the Receit of Reason
> A Lymbeck onely: when in Swinish sleepe,
> Their drenched Natures lyes as in a Death,
> What cannot you and I performe upon
> Th' unguarded Duncan?
> [I. VII. 61–70]

He has now been plunged into his element. She has quelled his thoughts of "good" and "ill" by giving him a problem he is only too capable of solving. He accepts the problem and with it has accepted, without speculation, its moral implications.

> Away, and mock the time with fairest show,
> False Face must hide what the false Heart
> doth know.
>
> [I. VII. 81–2]

We see, after this practical decision, a very different man. He is, in a sense, become a soldier again, exercising his proper craft. His wife has seized upon the one quality which is strong in him—his ability to execute that which is presented to him as a problem to be solved. Moral compunctions which had always been faint are overcome by a realisation that the task in hand is simple to execute. Lady Macbeth shows him this. Macbeth, it must be emphasised, is essentially a man of action. Like Othello he is most himself when *doing*, not thinking or feeling. The "influence" of the witches and Lady Macbeth upon him, combined, is categorically to place him in this correct element. When he says earlier that "Chance will have him king", he has to an extent given up. When Lady Macbeth points out that "chance" can be expedited by action, he is determined.

Yet, like Othello, this soldier is cursed by something that inhabits him, and which makes his status in the play far more profoundly subtle and powerful than that of mere brute, physical man. Macbeth is cursed by imagination. He can perform no deed without his mind eventually enlarging the consequences inside him. His wish that "this blow might be the be all and the end all here" is, considering his mental make-up, terribly ironic. The merely brute man commits murder with a present-tense access of physical violence; he does not have the imagination to project motive or consequence either backwards or forwards in time. Macbeth is saddled with the frightening ability both to remember and to foresee in images of engulfing power. In an artist this may be a blessing; in a man of action set upon a course of treacherous murder, it is a curse. In the famous soliloquy before he approaches

Duncan's chamber, the imagination is working in phase with the
present-tense actuality of the deed. The real dagger he is about to
use is also a dagger suspended in the chambers of his own mind.
The real steps he is taking must be unheard, otherwise they might
"prate" of his intentions, and denude the action of its implicit,
immediate, symbolism—horror. Yet, as soon as he returns from
the chamber his imagination begins to work in the past tense.
The effect is immensely impressive on our own sensibilities—
the man of action has begun now to be a victim of his curse.
He remembers a noise he heard; he recalls that one laughed
in his sleep, the other cried "murder", then "God bless us", then
"Amen". His memory pushes inwards upon him, like mounting
waves, knocking his words into a growing rhythm of imagined
guilt.

> Still it cry'd, Sleepe no more to all the House:
> Glamis hath murther'd Sleepe, and therefore Cawdor
> Shall sleepe no more: Macbeth shal sleepe no more.
> [II. II. 41-3]

It is important to note that this man of action has omitted an ele-
mentary precaution—to bring back the daggers from the murder
chamber. This is surely a measure of the extent to which the
imagination has accompanied and fractured the simplicity of
action during the present-tense performance of the deed. At this
point, two considerations must enter into critical estimation of
Macbeth's state.

The first concerns his realisation of his guilt. To what extent,
indeed, at this stage, has Macbeth a conscience? To the extent that
conscience implies regret at some deed committed which is subsequently wished uncommitted, he has a large one. In the murder
scene his huge imagination frightens his conscience into activity,
and the implications of the images it conjures up about a voice
saying that he shall sleep no more, about his bloody hands,
eventually come to mean one thing.

> Wake Duncan with thy knocking:
> I would thou could'st.
> [II. II. 73]

Yet Macbeth, at this point, does not have that kind of conscience which shows any pity for the victim of a deed committed. Indeed, far from regret over killing Duncan, the implication is that the real regret he feels is for himself and what the deed's implications have in store for him—moral compunctions have, by now, been entirely replaced by self-indulgent imagination.

The second important matter of interpretation at the point of Duncan's murder concerns, again, the nature of the relationship between Macbeth and his wife. It is customary to imagine them and, indeed, to depict them, as a closely-knit "fiend-like" duo. Indeed, they have sometimes been taken as representative of the idea that every great man, good or ill, should have, behind him, a woman of will and determination, urging him on. The extent of Lady Macbeth's urging has been noted; their mutual involvement in the crime is signified by Lady Macbeth's return to the chamber with the daggers and her reappearance with blood on her hands. Later, we are to see them together, and in the banquet scene she is to perform an act of tremendous will in holding together (if only just) her shattered husband. Yet, it is at the point of the murder where they are "but young in deed" that, paradoxically, these two begin to draw away from one another. Rather, Macbeth draws himself away from his wife. George Hunter writes of Macbeth's words immediately after Duncan's murder,

> The essential dialogue here is with himself; and Lady
> Macbeth, like other people in the play, remains accessory
> merely.[31]

This is true indeed and for the reasons that Hunter adds:

> The deed itself is a denial of all social obligations, all
> sharing, all community of feeling even with his wife.[32]

But the separation has another element in it as well. So far as the drawing away from Lady Macbeth is concerned, the simple fact is that she cannot follow him into the regions to which his imagination is taking him. As his imagination weaves around the words "Amen", "God bless us" and "sleep", pushing him into the final horror of:

> Will all great *Neptunes* Ocean wash this blood
> Cleane from my Hand?
>
> > [II. II. 60]

her responses are remarkably banal. "Consider it not so deeply". "What doe you meane?" She reveals her profound imaginative insensitivity when she says,

> . . . the sleeping, and the dead,
> Are but as Pictures: 'tis the Eye of Child-Hood
> That feares a painted Devill. If he doe bleed,
> Ile guild the Faces of the Groomes withall,
> For it must seeme their Guilt.
>
> > [II. II. 53–57]

And, if any doubts still remain that she is totally incapable of following Macbeth in his journey through hells of his own making, they would melt at her words:

> Retyre we to our Chamber:
> A little Water cleares us of this deed.
>
> > [II. II. 66–7]

This is an ironic reversal of Macbeth's belief that his hand will turn all the ocean to red.

Macbeth, then, becomes isolated from his society because of the deed, but isolated from individuals, even the closest to him, because he has a far greater imaginative power than they have. He is the loneliest of the four tragic heroes—utterly isolated on a sea of horrible imaginings whose shore on the one side encompasses the past, and, on the other, a limitless dark future. His eyes are sharp enough to see both simultaneously—he is terribly unique.

It is as if this access of loneliness which cloaks him at the death of Duncan also, paradoxically, gives him a new kind of strength. It may be observed that the Macbeth we see after Macduff has arrived to wake Duncan is not the tortured man of the previous scene. There is an icy kind of calm about him. In reply to questions and remarks, he is terse, as if screwing his courage up to a state of strength. "Good morrow both". "Not yet". "I'll bring you to him". "'Twas a rough night". He keeps his head while the discovery of the murder creates its own chaos and, in the end, takes charge of the situation.

> Let's briefely put on manly readinesse,
> And meet i' th' Hall together.
>
> [II. III. 133-4]

His possession of so much calm is the more remarkable in the face of the atmosphere of suspicion which his murder of the grooms has created. It is often unremarked that, in this and the following scene, Shakespeare, by hints, innuendoes, gives us a faint but ineradicable sense that Macbeth's action has not passed without bringing with it the whisper of suspicion. "Wherefore did you so?", inquires Macduff, and a little later phrases most curiously his answer to Ross's inquiry about who has done the deed—"Those that Macbeth hath slain". Even more pointed is Macduff's reply to Ross's disbelief that the two grooms could gain anything from murdering Duncan. He says,

> They were subborned,
> *Malcolme* and *Donalbaine* the Kings two sonnes
> Are stolne away and fled, which puts upon them
> Suspition of the deed.
>
> [II. IV. 24-26]

Suspicion has been "put upon them"—Macduff says no more on this score, but again most curiously phrases his answer to Ross's question.

> Then 'tis most like
> The Sovraignty will fall upon *Macbeth*
>
> [II. IV. 29-30]

He emphasises the haste with which the sovereignty has fallen upon him.

> He is already nam'd and gone to Scone
>
> [II. IV. 31]

There, he says, he will not go himself, though Macbeth's succession, in the face of the apparent treachery and defection of Malcolm, is legal. It is certainly remarkable that a senior Thane of high place will not go to see his new monarch's investiture. It is of course inviting danger, but more than this, his decision not to go, coupled with the implications of his remarks, emphasises a particular condition which, immediately after Duncan's murder, has entered into the play. Shakespeare is at pains to demonstrate that chaos, suspicion, and disorder has immediately fallen upon the society of which Macbeth has taken the head. The scene between Ross and the old man only serves to underline this. It is as if the deed has unlocked unnatural and dark forces—the fair times of Duncan have become foul almost within the hour; all has become unnatural "even like the deed that's done".

The range of Shakespeare's imaginative grasp of the meaning of evil is demonstrated superbly in this scene, and in Macduff's conversation with Ross. We have, up to now, seen evil as it corrodes and is embodied in one single man. This scene broadens the implications. The evil of one man, like that of Richard III, like that of Iago, corrupts a whole society. It is, so to say, only selective at first in its effects; it then spreads to bring about the disordering of a society as it has disordered one single individual. The general affiliations with the history plays are obvious, yet nowhere in these plays is there such a subtle interweaving of the effects of selective evil and of evil when on a total rampage. Where the *Henry VI* plays, and *Richard III*, cover large canvasses of time and space to show the growth of the forces of destruction and evil, *Macbeth* achieves it in an amazingly short space. The murder, its discovery, the comments upon it, the chaos it engenders, the unnatural portents which have accompanied it, are all gathered up into a virtual and terrible present tense, and in the near environs of where the deed occurred. Macbeth's earlier desire to have the deed and its consequences insulated within the present tense is here ironically counterpointed by a swift demonstration of those consequences.

The seeds of suspicion which Macduff seems to have in his mind are germinated for us some time after when he leaves for Fife, not Scone. Banquo's first words in Act Three are:

> Thou hast it now, King, Cawdor, Glamis, all,
> As the weyard Women promis'd, and I feare
> Thou playd'st most fowly for't.
>
> [III. I. 1–3]

Suspicion, disorder, have come to the surface. Where now does Macbeth stand?

First, his isolation is virtually complete; second, his acquisition of the throne has, from the very beginning, been attended by disorder, suspicion and, as we are told, a perplexed mind for himself and his queen. It is however to be remarked that so long as Macbeth can remain active, can at least give himself the illusion that he has some control over his destiny, he seems decisive, authoritative, and unswamped by imagination. So long as "fate" can be made to come unto the "list" he seems relatively calm and in command. He is courteously authoritative in the scene with Banquo before Banquo rides out for his last journey; he is scornfully in charge when he gives directions and probably lies to the two hired assassins. The possibility of action balances him. He has pulled himself together after the air-drawn dagger speech with the couplet:

> Heare it not, *Duncan*, for it is a Knell,
> That summons thee to Heaven, or to hell.
>
> [II. I. 63–4]

which is echoed in the couplet following the scene with the murderers:

> It is concluded: *Banquo*, thy Soules flight,
> If it find Heaven, must finde it out to Night.
>
> [III. I. 40–1]

It is as if the couplet, in itself, is an attempt to lock the acting of the deed into an unassailable, insulated present tense.

The extent to which the acquisition of kingship has given Macbeth a quality of decision is not commonly noted by critics, nor is it always communicated by actors. Neither Olivier nor Scofield,[33] the more recent distinguished interpreters of the part, caught this strain, which makes itself quite manifest in Act Three, scene two, when Lady Macbeth enters and asks him why he keeps himself so much to himself. The answer which she gets is clearheaded, rational. He knows exactly the position he is in, and knows, equally exactly, what his next step will be.

> Let your remembrance apply to *Banquo.*

Just as significant as this access of authority and rationality is a pronounced shift in the way in which his imagination works. He moves, for a time, from a state when it controls him, to a state when he seems able to call upon it, and exults in its power, and in his own ability to make it do what he asks. In a curious sense it is as if the fulfilment of his ambition (though it has cost him much) has strengthened the man. The irony is that his rationality, control, and authority suggest that, were all the circumstances different, he would have been an efficient and respected monarch.

> There's comfort yet, they are assaileable,
> Then be thou jocund:
>
> [III. II. 39–40]

This theoretical possibility is the more distinct when we see him at the beginning of the banquet scene. He is completely in command; he is gracious and regal.

> Our selfe will mingle with Society.
> And play the humble Host.
>
> [III. iv. 3–4]

It is very noticeable that even when the first murderer enters covertly to tell him that though Banquo is dead, Fleance still lives, Macbeth has only a moment of the old weakness; he loses control for an instant.

> But now I am cabin'd, crib'd confin'd, bound in
> To sawcy doubts and feares.
>
> [III. III. 24–5]

Yet he quickly recovers himself. He makes plans to talk further with the murderers, and returns to his guests; he even allows himself a wry remark about the absence of Banquo:

> Who, may I rather challenge for unKindnesse,
> Than pitty for Mischance.
>
> [III. IV. 42–3]

The "fit" which comes upon him with the appearance of Banquo's
ghost is, in effect, a struggle between the "new" rational Macbeth,
and the former weak, indecisive man, cursed by imagination.
The rhythmic movement of the scene is superbly controlled by
Shakespeare. The first wave knocks Macbeth out of sense.

> Thou canst not say I did it; never shake
> The goary lockes at me.
>
> [III. IV. 50–1]

The second wave plunges his mind into a cauldron of uncontroll-
able images

> Of Charnell houses, and our Graves must send
> Those that we bury, backe; our Monuments
> Shall be the Mawes of Kytes.
>
> [III. IV. 71–3]

> The times has bene,
> That when the Braines were out, the man would dye,
> And there an end.
>
> [III. IV. 78–80]

The third wave sucks all away, leaving him shattered but momen-
tarily restored to equilibrium.

> I do forget:
> Do not muse at me my most worthy Friends.
>
> [III. IV. 84–5]

With the return of the ghost comes the fourth wave, which causes
his mind, with a desperate anguish, to try and will this horrible
image into a shape and a situation which he can control—where he
can be truly himself and take action.

> Approach thou like the rugged Russian Beare,
> The arm'd Rhinoceros, or th' Hircan Tiger,

> Take any shape but that, and my firme Nerves
> Shall never tremble.
>
> [III. IV. 100–3]

The fifth wave is a return of the third—imagination overpowers
him; exhausted as he is, neither authority, will nor reason can hold
back the monstrous images.

> You make me strange
> Even to the disposition that I owe,
> When now I thinke you can behold such sights,
> And keepe the naturall Rubie of your Cheekes,
> When mine is blanch'd with feare.
>
> [III. IV. 112–15]

Finally, when all have left, this incredibly battered man returns to
some semblance of order within himself. He grasps again at the one
thing which is indigenous to him, which gives him equilibrium
and rationality—the possibility of action. The professional man,
shaking upon his legs, speaks.

> Strange things I have in head, that will to hand;
> Which must be acted, ere they may be scand.
>
> [III. IV. 139–40]

These two lines sum up Macbeth's personality. He is of that kind
whose disposition is to act and then to speculate. His curse and
tragedy is that his weak moral fibre, in combination with his
powerful imagination, confounds his will to control himself in
acting "rightly" or "wrongly".

His resolution to act takes him again to the witches. Here he is
presented with images which equal in intensity and implication
anything that he himself can conjure out of the resources of his
own imagination. He is shown the future and it appals him. Yet,
from the deep recesses of his mind, the impulse to contain the
future within the present tense—"If it were done when 'tis done"
—still works. After the witches disappear he says,

> Let this pernitious houre
> Stand aye accursed in the Kalendar.
>
> [IV. I. 133–4]

E

The future he has been shown is "pernicious", yet his mind tries
to confine it within an hour. When Lennox informs him
that Macduff is fled to England he remonstrates with Time for
having anticipated what he plans to do—he wants the deed and
its consequences to proceed together. He chastises Time for its
treachery.

> Time, thou anticipat'st my dread exploits:
> The flighty purpose never is o're-tooke
> Unlesse the deed go with it.
>
> [IV. I. 144–6]

Yet again, it is the thought of action that restores his equilibrium.
The words that announce this are significant:

> To Crown my thoughts with Acts: be it thoght and done.
>
> [IV. I. 49]

Speculation, act and consequence must become one.

Shakespeare's skill in counterpointing individual disorder with
social disorder is brilliantly demonstrated in the scenes that follow
this second visit to the witches. Any actor who plays the part must
welcome the break; what it achieves for the audience is twofold.
The results of spreading evil are seen, first, in a domestic and har-
rowing sense—the murder of Macduff's family—and, secondly, in
a political sense—the conversation between Malcolm and Macduff
in the court of England.

These scenes are most skilful examples of the two extremes of the
effects of evil—the personal tragedy, the political chaos and suspicion. The scene between Malcolm and Macduff, so often condemned as dull by commentators and implicitly judged as such by
directors who cut it down, is of immense importance in re-estab-
lishing the context of large disorder which had, for a time, become
dramatically subservient to the active analysis of the disorder
within Macbeth himself. Even more than this, it has an importance
in that its initial atmosphere of suspicion and dissension in the
State's high places is in direct and ironic contrast to the earlier
scenes of Duncan's court where all is amity, fidelity and order.
With the Malcolm/Macduff conversation, faint optimism and a

glimmer of order to come, enter again into the play. The rhythm of history once more asserts its power; this tragedy, in this scene and the ones that follow in which Scot and Englishman join to destroy evil, restores rightful degree and order, and confirms that Shakespeare's access of pessimism, revealed so darkly in *Troilus and Cressida*, had not defeated his inherent faith in an ordered universe. Within the terms of this play, the Lady Macduff scene, the Malcolm/Macduff confrontation, followed as they are by the whispered words between the Doctor and the Gentlewoman and Lady Macbeth's sleep-walking, play an essential part in emphasising the loneliness into which Macbeth has leaped by his deeds. During these scenes he is "lost" from the action; when we next see him he is utterly solitary.

> Those he commands, move onely in command,
> Nothing in love.
>
> [v. II. 19–20]

When we next see him he seems to be the inhabitant of an empty castle—the sense of empty dark space around him is extraordinary. No other tragic hero reveals quite this ultimate in separation from humanity, ordered society, love. Shakespeare intensifies the theatrical effect of this by giving him only two visible companions—the "lily-livered" Seyton and the Doctor who, were he "from Dunsinane away and clear,/Profit again should hardly draw" him there. It may be concluded that the inner loneliness of Macbeth's soul is now deliberately made visible as a result of Shakespeare's theatrical instincts. Where, we may ask, are Macbeth's forces? His "false Thanes" have fled. We are given an almost ridiculously frightening impression of a man determined to fight a whole army alone. Yet it is only "almost" ridiculous. At this point in the play, perhaps for the first time, we really feel twinges of pity for the man. He is determined to follow his instincts to act, but he is doing so upon the commission of a pathetically held faith in the equivocations of the witches. He has passed through moral compunctions, through indecision, through fear even. The irony is that, at last, he is in complete command of his imagination.

> I have almost forgot the taste of Feares:
> The time ha's beene, my sences would have cool'd
> To heare a Night-shrieke, and my Fell of haire
> Would at a dismall Treatise rowze, and stirre
> As life were in't. I have supt full with horrors,
> Direnesse familiar to my slaughterous thoughts
> Cannot once start me.
>
> [v. v. 9–15]

All he is capable of now is action; the death of his wife enables him, at last, to put his imagination to its final task—to assess the meaning of existence. Having done this, imagination itself dies—there is nothing more it can do since even its prophetic powers add up to nothing.

> Life's but a walking Shadow, a poore Player,
> That struts and frets his houre upon the Stage,
> And then is heard no more. It is a Tale
> Told by an Ideot, full of sound and fury
> Signifying nothing.
>
> [v. v. 24–8]

It is important to stress that with fear gone, imagination dispossessed, Macbeth is left with that one quality which, without ambition, without imagination, without moral weakness, might well have made him a man of greatness—the will to act. One by one the witches' equivocating prophecies are revealed for what they are, but at each withdrawal of illusory safety, Macbeth reacts by deciding to act.

> At least wee'l dye with Harnesse on our backe.
> [v. v. 52]

> But Bear-like I must fight the course.
> [v. vii. 2]

> Yet I will try the last. Before my body
> I throw my warlike Shield. Lay on, Macduffe,
> And damm'd be him, that first cries, hold, enough.
> [v. viii. 32–4]

Macbeth is often relegated to the status of "unsympathetic" tragic villain. His stark and violent butchery is put forward, in contrast to Hamlet's wavering, Othello's misguided pride, Lear's foolishness, as having no excuse with which to command any kind of admiration or pity from reader or audience. Yet, if we place him alongside Iago, who *seems* equally blandly and totally evil, can we in the final analysis relegate him to the role of mass murderer? We are forced to pause before placing them side by side in infamy. Throughout the whole play of *Macbeth*, but most notably in the early acts, there is surely a sense created that here is a man who could, most positively, be good and great. What we witness is a tragedy of the most painful, and yet pure kind—that of a man in whose personality there is a dissociation between certain characteristics which, in themselves, are potentially admirable. He has a will for action, a powerful imagination, self-knowledge, an ability to distinguish between good and evil, a strong awareness of love, fidelity and honour. As they are mixed by Shakespeare, in this play, what emerges is evil; but in the inevitability with which he surrounds himself with evil, and in the searing self-knowledge which accompanies it, Macbeth becomes a suffering man. Iago suffers nothing; his self-knowledge is a wry self-indulgence. His imagination is practical rather than transcendental.

It may be, too, that there is another quality about the character which absolves him from total condemnation. George Hunter remarks on the fact that though there is "nothing morally admirable about the capacity to speak well, we are in fact held sympathetically by a sense of surviving significance in his rhythms, even in those final speeches whose content is devoted to the meaninglessness of existence.[34] Macbeth's enormous desire to survive, his unabated capacity to take action in order so to do, in themselves elicit from us a feeling of, at the least, respect. More than this, the language through which he expresses his desire and his capacity is of a soul-searching eloquence. Such language in the service of good would order kingdoms and inspirit commonwealths. In the service of evil it astounds our minds and feelings by its power and its apparently limitless possibilities of invention. The "butcher" Macbeth confirms, paradoxically, the dignity of human communication.

The play is, to all intents and purposes, a one-man play. The theme of disorder painfully transmuted into order is present, but in the shadow of the spotlight which plays upon Macbeth. The characters which surround him play their roles but their position is entirely under the sway of Macbeth's presence. There is no greater measure or demonstration of this than the character of Lady Macbeth herself. Brave and great actresses have tried to find a "personality" within her which has a coherence and a validity in its own right—few of them seem to have succeeded. If we may believe an eye-witness account even the most famous of Lady Macbeths (Mrs Siddons) failed to find the interior of the character.

> Mrs Siddons was at first much agitated; in the scenes with Macbeth immediately brought before and after the murder of Duncan she was admirably expressive of the genuine sense and spirit of the author; but in the banquet scene in the third act, her abilities did not shine to so much lustre. In several passages of the dialogue she adopted too much the familiar manner, approaching to the comic; this may be called her epilogue style in which she has already experienced an entire failure. In this scene an exception must be made to her rebuke of Macbeth (though even that had not the powerful effect we might have expected from Mrs Siddons) and the congé to her guests, which last was delivered with inimitable grace.
>
> In the taper scene she was defective; her enunciation was too confined . . . the faces she made were horrid and even ugly, without being strictly just or expressive. She appeared in three several dresses. The first was handsome and neatly elegant, the second rich and splendid, but somewhat pantomimical, and the last one of the least becoming, to speak no worse of it, of any she ever wore upon the stage. Lady Macbeth is supposed to be asleep and not mad, so that custom itself cannot be alleged as a justification for her appearing in white satin.[35]

Mrs Siddons's own remarks on the character of Lady Macbeth seem to suggest the difficulties which she had in trying to find a centre to the character. She indulges in a whole series of generalisations and one feels that she finds it essential to impose something upon the character because she cannot find anything in the character itself which can grow inside her.

Lady Macbeth, like the rest, ministers to the presence of Macbeth. She is so small a creature by comparison with her husband. This is borne upon us with severe emphasis when we compare her "imagination" with his. Only once does she display anything comparable in the "creative" force of his imagination. This is in the soliloquy in which she calls upon the spirits to unsex her. On this occasion alone, she mounts beyond her normal and customary station. The woman we habitually see is devoid of the sensitivity or complexity of that kind of mental power which suggests either strong will or subtle imagination. It is easy for her (before Duncan's murder) to exhibit some willpower over her wavering husband. No deed has been committed up to this point. In fact, her mood at this time is one nearer to bravado than anything else. When the deed has been committed her lack of sensitivity shows. She believes a little water will clear them of the deed. Appallingly, and with apparent off-handedness, she says that she would have done it had not Duncan resembled her father. This statement is the key to her mental make-up. Macbeth haunts himself by the creative scope of his imagination. Lady Macbeth is destroyed by mere memory. Her mind can pre-figure nothing, but it is astonishingly retentive. What destroys her reason is her memory; she discovers the untruth of her own remark "what's done is done". In the banquet scene a courageous bravado again sees her through. She remembers the air-drawn dagger and dismisses it. Our next news of her is indirect, through the reports of the Doctor. It is clear, by now, that she has become a prey to memories which she cannot dismiss.

I have seen her rise from her bed, throw her
Night-Gown upon her, unlocke her Closset, take

foorth paper, folde it, write upon't, read it,
afterwards Seale it, and againe returne to bed.

[V. I. 1–5]

Is this a memory of a letter she wrote to her husband before the murder of Duncan? We do not know, but what she says during her sleep-walk suggests that images of palpable and concrete happennings from the past are dominant in her mind. She remembers the blood on her hands—"Out damned spot". She remembers Lady Macduff—"Where is she now?" She remembers Macbeth's susceptibilities—"You marre all with this starting". She remembers the smell of blood—"All the perfumes of Arabia will not sweeten this little hand". She remembers the night of the murder —"Wash your hands; put on your Night-Gowne; looke not so pale".

The accumulation of memories destroys Lady Macbeth. Being the sort of person whose imagination only works backwards, so to say, she is doomed to be isolated from a man whose imagination works in all directions of time and space. She is the smaller of the two for her limitations, and, perhaps, the more pitiful. She is, indeed, not fiend-like (certainly less so than Margaret of Anjou). Rather, she is a female with little sense of reason, no sense of morality. Her strength is typically womanly—the ability to put on a false face to hide what the false heart doth know. This is her bravado—countless women have displayed it to protect, even upon evil grounds, those whom they love.

Banquo is, theatrically speaking, a dull character. He comes, at one or two points, near to developing into an attractively interesting man, but Shakespeare, seemingly deliberately, stops him short. The first occasion is after the first appearance of the witches when he agrees "very gladly" to discuss what has happened at some future time; the second time is immediately before Duncan's murder when he is alone with his thoughts.

Mercifull Powers, restraine in me the cursed thoughts
That nature gives way to in repose.

[I. VII. 7–8]

How near, we wonder, are these cursed thoughts to Macbeth's? How near is Banquo to uttering them and, indeed, acting upon them? We are never allowed to know. He slips back to play his mechanistic role in the plot line, emerging only once more to give us hope that there is subtle mettle in him.

> Yet it was saide
> It should not stand in thy Posterity,
> But that my selfe should be the Roote, and Father
> Of many Kings. If there come truth from them,
> As upon thee *Macbeth*, their Speeches shine,
> Why be the verities on thee made good,
> May they not be my oracles as well,
> And set me up in hope.
>
> [III. I. 3–10]

Banquo is, at bottom, a conventionally good and honourable man, given just enough temptation to arouse in him unworthy thoughts and feelings. These are very intermittent but sufficient to give the action a touch of piquancy when they occur.

Macduff, again, is little more than an agency in the plot line. Arguments which have been conducted about the moral rightness or wrongness of his leaving his home and family at the mercy of Macbeth seem irrelevant. We are given too little evidence concerning the inside of Macduff to judge whether he is acting rightly or wrongly. The moments when an actor may find in the character sufficient to help him present a cogent characterisation are few and far between. The England scene between him and Malcolm gives some opportunity for a display of emotional variety, but even here, there is a curious negativeness about the man. He seems to respond automatically, to say exactly the right things, in reply to Malcolm's various tests of his integrity and purpose. This sense of automatic response is strong even in the scene where he learns of the murder of his wife and family. The scene is indeed infinitely touching yet, to some degree, we find it difficult to attach our pity to Macduff himself. It is as if he is a mere symbol and not the direct human recipient of grief. Macduff is an irritating character to an audience, and if we seek to find the source of our irritation, it must

surely lie in the fact that, by comparison with the man he eventually destroys, he seems wooden in intellect, lacking in imagination,
uncertain in motivation.

Duncan is constantly presented to us as an image of goodness.
Many of the qualities which Malcolm says he does not possess

> As Justice, Verity, Temp'rance, Stablenesse,
> Bounty, Perseverance, Mercy, Lowlinesse,
> Devotion, Patience, Courage, Fortitude,
>   [IV. III. 92–4]

Duncan is either expressly or implicitly shown to have. Shakespeare goes out of his way to keep this golden image before us even
after the murder. In the scene immediately ensuing the murder the
words "Duncan" "The king" "His Majesty" "royal master"
"royal father", toll continuously like a mournful bell through the
action. Subsequently, whenever Duncan is referred to, the image
presented is always in stark contrast to the present-tense actuality
of Macbeth's reign. His body goes to "the sacred storehouse of his
predecessors". Macbeth calls him "gracious Duncan"; "after life's
fitful fever he sleeps well". We are never allowed to forget this
man. In no other tragedy of Shakespeare's is there such a consistent
implied and direct opposition made between good and evil as in
this opposition between the actuality and image of Duncan, and the
actuality of Macbeth.

His son, Malcolm, whose elevation as Prince of Cumberland
gives Macbeth his first speculations about the barriers to be overcome for the fulfilment of the prophecies, ought to be a glowing
dramatic figure in the play, but is not. All there is of him may be
summed up in the word "representative". He is representative of
the forces of order which will restore peace to Scotland; he is representative of the orderly progression of dynasty, rudely interrupted
by Macbeth; even the doubts which he plants in Macduff's mind
about his fitness to be king strike us more as representative of an
argument Shakespeare wants to introduce at this point, than as an
inevitable embodiment of his own speculative nature. An actor
has, virtually, to "make" a character out of Malcolm because
there is so little positive to interpret. A recent example of such

making is interesting, both for the solution it attempts and also because the attempt has necessarily involved the manufacturing of "characteristics" for Malcolm whose existence in the text itself are in some cases barely apparent, and in others unsupported. Nevertheless it is, in face of the character as he stands, a shrewd attempt.

> Malcolm is not the sweet, young, good, holier-than-thou
> hero that everybody thinks he is. In the England scene
> when he talks about the wives, daughters, his lust and desire,
> he is putting on a pretty good show to test Macduff. But it
> is such a good show because, like all men who are correctly
> moulded for power, he probably has, deep down inside him,
> a considerable amount of megalomania. The power to have
> women, money, to "uprear the universal peace" and to
> "pour the sweet milk of concord into hell", although he is
> over-dramatising it, suggests that deep down inside he has a
> slight conscious knowledge of the possibilities of something
> bad like that in himself. The reason why he seems good and
> tends to be a little holier-than-thou is because he is aware of
> the weakness that is in himself, and in the people he deals
> with. He is a virgin, therefore all the things that he says he
> will do with women are a sort of masturbatory fancy;
> similarly all the things he says about power and wealth must
> be a knowledge of the megalomania that is in him.[36]

Would indeed that the character of Malcolm in Shakespeare's play were as interesting as this interpretation.

In the end all the characters pale into insignificance in comparison with Macbeth himself. The curious fact is that whatever moral judgements one makes on him, whatever allowance of sympathy one is prepared to grant or to withhold, he cannot be forced out of one's imagination, as Kemble noted:

> In the performance on the stage, the valour of the tyrant,
> hateful as he is, invariably commands the admiration of every
> spectator of the play.[37]

It is as if Shakespeare's theatrical power exerts such a fascination on us that, in the final analysis, it weakens any disposition we have to question intellectually the moral pattern of the play. Chaos is expunged in the end, order re-asserts itself, the commonwealth, tested sorely by evil, is brought back to health. Yet it is not this that we remember when we leave the book or the performance. We remember only that we have experienced, as John Wain says,

> Not so much with our visual imagination as with our hands, teeth, throats, our very skin, hair and nails,[38]

the ultimate example of the way in which a fiction may be made terrifyingly real.

3

A PROBLEM TRAGEDY:

Timon of Athens

Timon of Athens is, in many ways, one of Shakespeare's strangest plays. Doubts have frequently been voiced about the extent of Shakespeare's hand in it and indeed about whether he had anything to do with it at all. It cannot confidently be described by any other word than tragedy, yet it seems conspicuously out of key with the other tragedies. Its inclusion in the first Folio, where it is placed in the tragedies section between *Romeo and Juliet* and *Julius Caesar*, is surrounded with problems. It is now generally agreed that this position was originally reserved for *Troilus and Cressida* but because for some reason that play was unavailable for printing, a hurried substitution of a play roughly capable of fitting in the vacant space was made. The rough calculations were wrong and the printer found himself with the need to leave out a whole quire of paper. The result, in the printed Folio, is that there is a gap between pages 98 and 109, one completely blank page and the insertion of another that had obviously been reserved for the names of those who acted the play originally.

The date of composition is not known with any exactness but a consensus of opinion would put it somewhere between 1605 and 1609. It certainly seems to fall towards the end of the great period of tragic plays.

The problems mentioned so far pale into insignificance beside the textual inconsistencies, and the irregularities of verse, theme and character with which it abounds. Johnson[1] found that "there are many passages perplexed, obscure, and probably corrupt", and although certain critics have expressed enthusiasm for it—notably Coleridge, Hazlitt and, more recently, Wilson Knight[2]—overall its acceptance by both critics and audiences has been less than enthusiastic. It is probably the least performed of the plays, with the possible exception of *Pericles*.

And yet, for all this the play, seemingly so remote in tone from its immediate context in the canon of the plays, and apparently so unattractive to so many directors, actors and critics, has one characteristic which should engage the attention of the late twentieth century—one strong enough, indeed, to induce a guess that it is on the threshold of revival.

No other play of Shakespeare's expresses with such directness, a set of attitudes which seems so germane to many of the intellectual, emotional and moral preoccupations of many people today, particularly that significant minority who both fear and care for the condition of our Western civilisation. *Timon of Athens* is—and this is curiously ironic—one of Shakespeare's apparently most uncharacteristic plays and yet one of the most apposite to our times.

In several major respects the play differs from the four great tragedies. The most obvious may be described as one of genre. The other tragedies may be termed as essentially realistic plays. What they communicate, and the "psychological" being of the characters are both verifiable, as it were, in terms of our experience of real life. There is a sense in which we believe that their events and situations actually occur and that their characters are living human beings.

This is not the case with *Timon of Athens*, although the protagonist was in fact a real historical figure who is mentioned in Plutarch's *Lives*.[3] There is more credibility in the existence of a historical Timon than there is in that of a Hamlet or a Lear, but the dramatised version created by Shakespeare is far less credible. If the other tragedies may, for convenience, be given the label of "realistic" the term most apparently applicable to this play is "allegorical". It suggests this description not only because the reader or theatregoer has a persistent sense that personification is being used for the communication of abstract ideas, but also because of the presence of that kind of constructional symmetry, of imposed pattern, often to be found in allegorical work. The other tragedies proceed to their conclusions with a relentless and realistic inevitability, but *Timon's* conclusion seems already intellectually established before the play begins and what we see is an allegorical demonstration of how that conclusion was reached. The personification involved is not as absolute as, for example, in the highly-wrought *Faerie Queene* of Spenser, but it is unmistakably present. The play's "idea", its central core, is concerned with enforcing a moral conclusion upon its readers or viewers. It has a "message" for us about what we are like, how we behave to each other, about our sense of values. What happens in the play to the characters, and what is said by them, are in a very strict respect, fashioned for little more than the function of enforcing this abstract message. Even Timon, obviously the most highly developed dramatically speaking, seems cabin'd, cribbed and confined when set alongside the free-ranging dramatic existence of the four great tragic heroes. Others, particularly the painter, the poet and the senators and, to a lesser extent, Alcibiades and Apemantus, are personifications of attitudes. Their place in the system of the play in this respect can be clearly understood when it is recalled that in the final act Timon's visitors in his self-imposed exile are representative of the military (Alcibiades) philosophy (Apemantus) the visual arts (the painter), the verbal arts (the poet), and the political world (two senators). The only significant absentees in this allegorical parade are the church and music. There is no priest to shrive and salve and no music (so often the balm of hurt minds in Shakespeare) to soothe and hasten a broken spirit towards concord. Inexorably, these representatives who visit Timon are used as examples of man's inhumanity, his cupidity, his hypocrisy or his simple *naïveté*—for Alcibiades is less a villain than a well-meaning innocent in his brashly simple military way.

This allegorical plan upon which it seems to have been built is reinforced, in one's mind, by a consideration of its actual construction. It is one thing to condemn it, as many commentators have done, for its inconsistencies of characterisation, for its lack of dramatic development, in terms both of incident and character, but quite another to ignore what seems, at the least, to be a strong pursuit by the author of symmetry. All the visitors to Timon (with the exception of Alcibiades) in Act five have already visited him, in his days of affluent but mindless generosity, in Acts one and two. In the early visits we experience something similar to the effects of Ben Jonson's satirical melodramas—a wry, satirical comment on social behaviour and an awareness that we are far more conscious of the truth behind what is really happening than some of the leading characters. In the later visits we experience not satire's *double-entendre*—laughter galled by distaste—but the deliberately unambiguous fact of moral turpitude. Whereas, in the first instance, we could shake our heads sagely while we smiled or laughed at Timon's gullibility in the face of the world's perfidy, in the second instance we are frozen into a recognition of the unalloyed hypocrisy of mankind.

Yet, such is the force of the allegorical mode as opposed to the realistic, that these experiences are largely intellectual, in our heads, so to say. What we think of them is of the same order as if we had been made to ponder on the perils of ambition without materially being affected by the presence of Macbeth in the play. The poet, the painter, even the senators, are not individualised and the frisson their presence gives us is more of head than of heart, simply because we are not asked to be engaged with them in a sense which is even approximately human.

It is this creation of an allegorical equation, as distinct from a dramatic reality, which marks this play off fundamentally from the four great tragedies. The isolation of Timon (in contradistinction to that of his tragic colleagues) seems more an artificial imposition than a natural outcome of event and personality. The society around Timon, although its rotted values can, in an intellectual sense, be taken as emblematic of mankind in general, does not have that quality of actuality so typical of the tragedies. Indeed it is not merely actuality that is at a premium but that characteristic and unique relationship between the protagonist and his social context. Macbeth's perfidy becomes Scotland's ruin; Hamlet's and Elsinore's descent are inexorably connected; the darkness and chaos that come to inhabit Lear's mind have their intimates in the darkness and chaos that descend upon his country; what Iago works upon Othello's imagination and spirit affects the lives of others in the society about him. Yet what happens to Timon, both outwardly and inwardly, seems curiously insulated, self-contained. It is as if we might say that, in dramatic and theatrical terms, the character is created to have a singularity that completely isolates him. This play does not, as the other tragedies do, maintain and develop the huge dimension of that great theme of the interdependence of inner and outer order and disorder which began in the early histories and reached one peak in the great tragedies.

The question arises as to why the play should be so manifestly of a different order of tragedy from its fellows. The temptation always exists to attribute such obvious departures to a persistent spirit of experimentation in Shakespeare. Where *Cymbeline* (a somewhat later play) is concerned, this explanation for its differences from the typical Shakespearean romance drama has good and wide currency, though it should be warned that the reasons offered by scholars for this experimentation and indeed their assessments of the value of the end-product are extremely diverse.

At first sight the evidence already adduced of a pursuit of symmetry might seem to provide the keystone clue to the argument that *Timon of Athens* was an experimental play. The difficulty, however, is that if one is looking for evidence pointing to an expected result there is the greatest danger of assuming that we know what the clue really means and that we accept what we think it means in order to achieve this result.

The presence of an urge to symmetry could very well argue for a quite different explanation.

Timon of Athens is believed by a few to be the work of a hand other than Shakespeare's, by some to be partly his and by more to be his entirely. There is a formidable weight of scholarship on the side of concluding that the text as printed in the first Folio is from Shakespeare's foul papers (i.e. a first uncorrected manuscript draft). If we assume this then it could feasibly account for the simple symmetry of the play and for the allegorical colouring. The tendency of the first "blocking" of a play or a novel by an author is towards a balancing of forces. The initial thrust is towards giving equal value to the constituent parts already decided upon. It is only in the later stages of writing that a more creatively fecund process of judicious unbalancing takes place—the result of this second procedure is to denude the work of its original mechanical appearance. Obvious constructional symmetry tends to disappear, to be replaced by a far more subtle architecture.

So far as allegorising is concerned the tendency in creating character is first to write down what a character is, or represents. In a world demanding, as the Elizabethan theatre did or as the modern best-seller world does, quick "turnover", it is almost inevitable that character, in a first draft, tends to be divided into "good" and "bad"; the subtleties come later. Clearly, if the characterisation remains in this first state of creation, the emphasis will be less on individuality than on representativeness—a condition tending to the allegorical.

This process is strikingly illustrated in the words of a contemporary best-selling novelist—Alistair MacLean.[4] He describes his first "blocking" process.

> First I drew up a list of the characters and then I drew a diagram of the plot. There were circles to show where the characters came in and red crosses to show where they died. Then I looked at it again and said, "MacLean, you've got the balance wrong—too many crosses in the middle and not enough at the end", so I rearranged it until there were crosses all the way through.

Without suggesting that this was the method used by Shakespeare, it should be noted that the evidence of writers in notebooks and letters over the centuries indicates that the first drafts of works often have this urge to the symmetrical and what, in fact, might be called the accidentally allegorical.

Some of the curiosities in the text of the play may be due to the fact that Shakespeare's foul papers had, in part, been transcribed by a man who seems to have played a shadowy but important part in the preparation of the first Folio for printing. Ralph Crane was a scrivener who worked for the legal profession but is widely believed to have been responsible for transcribing *The Merry Wives of Windsor, The Two Gentlemen of Verona, Measure for Measure, The Winter's Tale* and *The Tempest* for the press. Crane's work may have gone beyond transcribing and involved a deal of editing. The editor[5] of a modern edition gives examples of Crane's work:

> ... "ha's" for both "he has" and "has" and "em" for "them", his curious use of apostrophes in phrases like "I'am" and "ye'have", and his fondness for hyphens colons and parentheses. ...

How far an early draft, multiple authorship or scribal and editorial interference are responsible for what seems like an unfinished play cannot be decided. *Timon of Athens* clearly lacks the sense of finish (even allowing for the exigencies of the Elizabethan printing trade) of the majority of Shakespeare's plays. The subplot is curiously separate from the main plot and does not "join" with it until Act four, scene three. The part played by women is minimal (a strange process for Shakespeare) yet there are hints that one or more were originally intended to be developed characters, particularly in IV, iii when Timon addresses one of Alcibiades' harlots by name. The language of the play, too, veers between occasionally quite superb utterance and rough, uncut speech. The dramatic and psychological rightness of:

> They answer in a joynt and corporate voice,
> That now they are at fall, want Treasure
> cannot do what they would, are sorrie: you are Honourable,
> But yet they could have wisht, they know not,
> Something hath beene amisse; a Noble Nature
> May catch a wrench; would all were well; tis pity,
> And so intending other serious matters,
> After distastefull lookes; and these hard Fractions
> With certaine halfe-caps, and cold moving nods,
> They frose me into silence.

in which the Steward keenly impersonates the various excuses of

Timon's alleged friends is counterbalanced by the thick-tongued ineptitude of:

>   They confesse
>   Toward thee, forgetfullnesse too generall grosse;
>   Which now the publike Body, which doth sildome
>   Play the re-canter, feeling in it selfe
>   A lack of *Timons* ayde, hath since withall
>   Of it owne fall, restraining ayde to Timon,
>   And send forth us, to make their sorrowed render,
>   Together, with a recompence more fruitfull
>   Then their offence can weigh downe by the Dramme. . . .

There are inconsistencies not only in the play but in the character of Timon. His remoteness from the powerful realism of the tragic heroes is emphasised by the means with which he is first brought to our acquaintance. We become aware of him less as a dramatic agent than as a kind of emblem.

>   *Poet:* Nay Sir, but heare me on:
>   All those which were his Fellowes but of late,
>   Some better than his valew; on the moment
>   Follow his strides, his Lobbies fill with tendance,
>   Raine Sacrificiall whisperings in his eare,
>   Make Sacred even his styrrop, and through him
>   Drinke the free Ayre.
>
>   .   .   .   .
>
>   When Fortune in her shift and change of mood
>   Spurnes downe her late beloved; all his Dependants
>   Which labour's after him to the Mountaines top,
>   Even on their knees and hand, let him sit downe,
>   Not one accompanying his declining foot.

When Timon does impinge on us in less emblematic guise what is dominant in his character seems to be extravagance and gullibility. Unless the word "noble" is stretched to an extent beyond what would seem reasonable then H. J. Oliver's[6] description of Timon smacks more of an excuse than a truly critical delineation. He writes of him as a man of "noble generosity". But there is surely

little need for Shakespeare's obvious intentions in the early
scenes of this play to be subjected to the kind of softening implied
in that phrase. These scenes, in which we meet the Athenian estab-
lishment of which Timon is a part, show us first the sycophancy,
expediency, calculated responses and moral bankruptcy of this
society, and second the self-indulgent, self-deluding expense of
wealth and spirit in a waste of shame of Timon who, after all, is
attempting to hold this society to him. If it be noble to spend one's
substance to keep the good offices and report of such a society as
this then the Arden editor is right, though it must still be remembered that Timon's generosity depends on borrowed money. If
this is to be noble then we have to seek out sweeter adjectives than
critical assessment would normally apply to, for example, characters like Iachimo, Don John and others.

   In truth Shakespeare in these early scenes shows us just that seg-
ment of sophisticated "in" society life which would be most read-
ily recognised by twentieth-century readers and audiences. The
scenes give off the odour that can so often be experienced at those
unspeakable parties where the riff-raff, the failures, the crawlers of
the artistic world manage to insert themselves and hobnob with the
aristocracy, the well-lined or the famed—and will continue to
hobnob, just so long as there is a hint of irresponsible patronage in
the air. The modern world of mass-communications harbours such
things and, it is understood, they are not unknown in the world of
publishing.

   Timon is tarred with the same brush that is to be found in such
coteries. He is defiled and his responses, far from noble, put him in
a position to be defiled even more. His gullibility is stressed.

> I. Lord: Might but we have that happinesse my Lord,
>   that you would once use our hearts, whereby we
>   might expresse some part of our zeales, we should
>   thinke our selves for ever perfect.
> Timon: Oh no doubt my good Friends, but the Gods
>   themselves have provided that I shall have much
>   helpe from you: how had you beene my Friends else.

Apemantus is not fooled by the surrounding sycophancy—

"Would all those Flatterers were thine Enemies then, that the
thou might'st kill'em."

Timon is a long way from the mould from which the great
tragic heroes came. They all have a nobility at the outset or, at
least, a justifiable proudness (as opposed to "pride") as in the case
of Othello. Their nobility is not a small thing; in Hamlet is rests
upon moral complexity, intellectual and imaginative strength, in
Lear it shows itself in will and mental courage, in Macbeth it is
implicit in his military prowess. Timon is merely recklessly gener-
ous. It has been argued that the kind of largesse he displays would
have been regarded as natural and desirable in a renaissance world.
G. R. Hibbard[7] amplifies this graphically.

> . . . he goes in for the "conspicuous consumption" which
> became such a pronounced feature of upper-class life in
> England during the last twenty years or so of Elizabeth's
> reign and continued under her successor. There was a pas-
> sion for building new and elaborate houses; men appeared
> at court with "whole manors on their backs" in the form of
> rich clothes; they put on lavish and spectacular shows for
> their sovereign; they began to spend part of each year in
> London; and they went in for the gentlemanly vice of
> gaming. Seeking to live up to two ideals of conduct, both
> expensive, at the same time, the great frequently found
> themselves short of ready money, and proceeded to
> borrow it.

The fact that Timon is such a man does not, of course, render him
noble nor does it mean that the majority of Elizabethans were
prepared to condone behaviour which was meant to indicate to an
astonished world that you had arrived. Hibbard says that, to "the
moralists, the preachers, the poets, and the playwrights, it seemed
that human beings and human values were being sacrificed on
the altar of gain". Here, of course is yet another reason why this
play has a peculiarly contemporary tang to it. The headlong dash
of Western civilisation into the maw of materialism is mirrored
vividly in this play. It is to the disadvantage of the twentieth

century that it has no Francis Bacon to utter warnings. His words are apposite to Timon's case.

> Riches are for spending, and spending for honour and good actions—therefore extraordinary expense must be limited by the worth of the occasion.[8]

Timon suffers the fate which Bacon considers reserved for profligacy—"costly followers are not to be liked" lest, while a man maketh his train longer, he make his wings shorter".[9]

Timon of Athens is less a play than a kind of dramatised argument conducted by the protagonist with himself and with others. The logic of the argument is unclear but it is certainly concerned with the despicable condition of man and the equivocal part played by wealth in man's life. The detritus of what might have been an unusual theme can be discerned in various parts of the play, and in so far as it is possible to recognise specific features, two particular elements are worth commenting upon. The first is to do with the attitudes taken up by Timon and others towards money and the second is the way in which the servant characters are presented.

The language of the play is full of references to buying and selling, to what is mercantile and assessable in material terms. Friendship is measured in terms of how it can be bought and kept by the giving of gifts. It is only when the means by which so-called friendship is thus obtained have disappeared that Timon begins to realise the falseness of the ground upon which he has stood. He rails, however, not about his own faults, but about mankind.

Behind this demonstration of the change in Timon there lies an attitude towards richness and poverty which, for Shakespeare, is given an unusual stress. At first, mainly through the servants, what is emphasised is the misery of poverty—"thus part we rich in sorrow, parting poor", but this shifts to an underlining of the misery of affluence. The steward says,

> Who would not wish to be from wealth exempt,
> Since Riches point to Misery and Contempt?

The speech in which these lines occur is immediately followed by Timon's long harangue to himself in which he deplores the fact that it is mere chance which makes one man rich and another poor. These are curious sentiments to find written in an age when the acquisition of wealth and position was regarded as a most laudable ambition. Perhaps even more surprising is the sharp distinction made between the treatment of Timon by his alleged friends, and by his servants. The former are treacherous, the latter, particularly the Steward, are honourable. The distinction is almost mechanical in its appearance, as if the dramatist is bent on forcing a moral.

Indeed, the part played by servants in the play is unusually prominent. It would be very easy for a Marxist to read into this a justification of his own faith in the superior fidelity and honour of those who toil as opposed to those who merely acquire. Curiously, it would be equally easy for a Christian to regard the play as a demonstration of the words "Blessed be ye poor, for yours is the kingdom of God".

Yet, we are for ever denied knowledge of both the motivation and the precise meaning of this play. It is bitter, cynical, angry. It is, for Shakespeare, uncharacteristically deep in its pessimism and yet it is difficult to escape the feeling that his hand is in it. Perhaps the possessor of that hand had been, for a short time, weary of the world. Some things in it have the true ring of Shakespeare—perhaps they also reflect a temporary malaise of his spirit.

> My long sicknesse
> Of Health, and Living, now begins to mend,
> And nothing brings me all things.

REFERENCES

CHAPTER I

1. See 1.1., particularly Slender's remark—"they may give the dozen white Luces in their Coate".
2. For an account of Sir Edward Greville's part in the unrest see F. E. Halliday, *The Life of Shakespeare*, 1964, *passim*.
3. Extract from the will of Thomas Whittington, Mar. 25 1601, quoted in E. K. Chambers and C. Williams, *A Short life of Shakespeare*, 1933, p. 141.
4. Halliday, op. cit., p. 160.
5. See my account in *Shakespeare II*, 1969, pp. 13–14.
6. J. Dover Wilson, *The Essential Shakespeare*, 1937, p. 105.
7. *Ibid.*, p. 105.
8. *Ibid.*, p. 107.
9. *Ibid.*, p. 107.
10. The poem made its first appearance in a group of commendatory verses attached to a long poem, *Loves Martyr or Rosalins Complaint*, by Robert Chester, first published in 1601.
11. Towards the end of Elizabeth's reign the boys' companies, which had earlier developed from choir schools and were commissioned to act in court pageants, masques and ceremonies, became professionally organised and performed outside court. The Children of Paul's and the Children of the Chapel were the most popular and successful troupes.
12. Philip Henslowe (d. 1616). A Devon man who, before entering theatre management, appears to have been a jack of all trades—dyer and pawnbroker included. With his interests in bear-baiting and commercial theatre he became the most powerful businessman in London's entertainment world. See particularly R. A. Foakes and R. T. Rickert (eds),

Henslowe's Diary, 1961, one of the chief sources of information about the Elizabethan theatre.

13. In the epistle to Anthony Scoloker, *Daiphantus, or the Passions of Love*, 1604.

14. Thomas Kyd (1558–94), a contemporary of Edmund Spenser at Merchant Taylors' school. His play, *The Spanish Tragedy* (first performed *c.* 1599) ran to ten known editions between 1592 and 1633. It was probably the most famous of all Elizabethan revenge plays. Ironically, Kyd's name appears on none of the ten title pages.

15. For a Facsimile, translation and discussion of this fascinating document which is, apart from connections with Shakespeare, important as a piece of social history, see B. Roland Lewis (ed.), *Shakespeare Documents*, 1940, Vol. 2, pp. 329–36.

16. *Ibid.*, p. 415.

17. *Ibid.*, p. 364.

18. E. K. Chambers, *William Shakespeare*, 1930, pp. 113–14.

19. B. Roland Lewis, p. 371.

CHAPTER 2

1. Thomas Rymer, *A Short View of Tragedy*, 1693, conveniently quoted in F. E. Halliday, *Shakespeare and his Critics*, 1958, p. 61.

2. From the preface to Alexander Pope's edition of Shakespeare of 1725. Again, quoted in Halliday, p. 63.

3. See, for example, T. Spencer, *Shakespeare and the Nature of Man*, 1942; J. Danby, *Shakespeare's Doctrine of Nature*, 1949; R. Sewall, *The Vision of Tragedy*, 1959; W. Farnham, *The Medieval Heritage of Elizabethan Tragedy*, 1936.

4. Irving first performed Hamlet at the Lyceum Theatre on 31 Oct. 1874.

5. M. L. Mare and W. H. Quarrell (trans.) *Lichtenberg's Visits to England as Described in His Letters and Diaries*, 1938. Conveniently quoted in Richard Findlater, *The Player Kings*, 1971, pp. 45–6. See also Gareth LLoyd Evans, *Shakespeare in the Limelight*, 1968, p. 38 *passim.*

6. See Harley Granville Barker's views on this point in *Prefaces to Shakespeare*, 1960.

7. *Ibid.*, p. 29.

8. See Gareth LLoyd Evans, *Shakespeare II*, 1969, p. 13 *passim*.

9. R. W. Chambers, *Man's Unconquerable Mind*, 1950, p. 46.

10. B. Ifor Evans, *The Language of Shakespeare's Plays*, 1952, p. 105.

11. E. Wilson (ed.) *Shaw on Shakespeare*, 1969, pp. 102–3.

12. Cinthio (Giovanni Battista Giraldi) 1504–73. Italian novelist and dramatist. His *Hecatommithi* (*c.* 1565) is a series of prose-tales linked by a narration which is supposed to occur aboard ship.

13. H. H. Furness (ed.) *Othello*, Variorum Shakespeare, 1886, p. 377.

14. O. J. Campbell and E. G. Quinn (eds.) *A Shakespeare Encyclopaedia*, 1966, p. 599.

15. Furness, p. 395.

16. *Ibid.*

17. *Ibid.*, p. 393.

18. K. Muir (ed.) *Othello*, 1968, p. 17.

19. *Ibid.*

20. *Ibid.*, p. 12.

21. Harley Granville Barker, *Prefaces to Shakespeare*, 1963, p. 266.

22. Muir, p. 44.

23. H. H. Furness (ed.) *King Lear*, Variorum Shakespeare, 1880, p. 423.

24. Unsigned review in *Birmingham Spectator,* Sept 15th, 1825.

25. See the introductions to Furness, *op. cit.*

26. Hazlitt on Kean's King Lear in *The London Magazine*, June, 1820.

27. G. Wilson Knight, *The Wheel of Fire*, 1930, p. 57.

28. For a comprehensive study of this view see Wilson Knight *op. cit.*

29. See Dennis Bartholomeusz, *Macbeth and the Players*, 1969, *passim*.

30. G. K. Hunter (ed.) *Macbeth*, New Penguin Shakespeare, 1967, p. II.

31. *Ibid.*, p. 16.
32. *Ibid.*, p. 17.
33. Laurence Olivier at the Shakespeare Memorial Theatre, 1955, and Paul Scofield at the Royal Shakespeare Theatre, 1968.
34. Hunter, p. 28.
35. John Taylor, *The Morning Post*, 3rd. Feb. 1785.
36. Ian Richardson in a tape-recorded interview with the author, 1969.
37. J. P. Kemble, *Macbeth Reconsidered*, 1786. Conveniently quoted in Bartholomeusz, *op. cit.*, p. 136 and *passim*.
38. John Wain, *The Living World of Shakespeare*, 1966, p. 212.

Chapter 3

1. In his notes to his edition of Shakespeare, 1765. The comment is conveniently reprinted in W. K. Wimsatt, *Dr. Johnson on Shakespeare*, 1969, p. 127.
2. G. Wilson Knight, *The Wheel of Fire*, 1930.
3. Reprinted in T. J. B. Spencer, *Shakespeare's Plutarch*, 1968.
4. In an article in *The Observer Magazine*, 1971, p. 14.
5. H. J. Oliver (ed.) *Timon of Athens*, The Arden Shakespeare, 1959, pp. XIX–XX.
6. *Ibid.*, p. XLIII.
7. G. R. Hibbard (ed.) *Timon of Athens*, New Penguin Shakespeare, 1970, pp. 33–4.
8. Francis Bacon, *Of Followers and Friends*, in *Essays or Counsels Civil and Moral*, 1597.
9. *Ibid.*, *Of Expense*.